The Wounded Spirit

Frank Peretti

WORD PUBLISHING

NASHVILLE

A Thomas Nelson Company

Library of Congress Cataloging-in-Publication Data

[applied for]

Printed in the United States of America

00 01 02 03 04 05 BVG 6 5 4 3 2 1

To Mom and Dad, whose love and encouragement never wavered, and to John, who stood on the wall.

Contents

Boy's Hell

Chapter One

A separate room had been prepared for the boys. It was cold and impersonal, like a prison; the echoing, concrete walls had been painted dirty beige, then marred and chipped over the years, then painted again. The walls were bare except for posted rules, warnings, and advisories, and the only windows were high against the ceiling, caged behind iron grillwork thickly wrapped in paint, rust, and more paint. The air was dank, tainted with the odors of steam, sweat, and skin. Years of rust and sediment from the dripping showerheads and armies of bare, wet feet had marbled the floor with streaks and patches of reddish brown.

The authorities, clad in uniforms and carrying clipboards and whistles, marched the boys in, at least forty of them, all roughly the same age but many different sizes, strengths, and physical maturities. The dates of their births, the locations of their homes, and the simple luck of the draw had brought them here, and much like cattle earmarked for shipment, they had no voice in the matter. The paperwork was in. This room would be a part of their lives for the next four years.

He had never been in this place, or anywhere like this place, before. He had never imagined such a place could even exist. In here, kindness meant weakness, human warmth was a complication, and encouragement was unmanly. In here, harshness was the guiding virtue—harshness, cruelty, and the blunt, relentless confirmation of every doubt he'd ever carried about himself.

Mr. M, a fearsome authority figure with a permanent scowl and a voice that yelled—only yelled—ordered them to strip down. His assistants, clones of his cruelty, repeated the order, striding up and down the narrow aisles between the lockers.

The boy hesitated, looking furtively about. He'd never been naked in front of strangers before, but even worse, he'd never been naked in front of enemies. It took only one class hour for the others to select him, to label him, and to put him in his place. He was now officially the smallest one, the scared one, the weakling, the one without friends. That made him fair game.

And now he would be naked in front of them. Naked. His stomach wrung; his hands trembled. *Dear God, please get me out of here. Please don't let them do this to me.*

But every authority figure in his life said he had to be here. He had to go to school, do his chores, finish his homework, keep his shoes tied, go to bed and get up at certain hours, eat his vegetables, and be here. End of discussion.

He removed his clothes.

Mr. M continued his yelling. "Come on, move it, move it, move it!"

The herd—pink, black, brown, and bronze—moved one direction, and all he could do was move with it, a frail, naked body among the forty, longing for a towel, anything to cover himself. Instinctively, he placed his hand over his private parts. Every other body was bigger and much stronger, and every other body had hair where the boy had none. He knew they would notice.

The showers were a long, high-ceilinged echo chamber, murky with steam, rattling with lewd, raucous joking and laughter. He didn't want to hear it.

After a big Hispanic kid finished his shower, the boy carefully took his place under the showerhead, afraid of slipping and even more afraid of grazing against anyone. Touching was dangerous; it could easily become a prelude to being hurt.

He let the water spray over him. He hurriedly lathered his body with some soap.

To his left, the talk started—about him. Then some laughing. The talk spread, the call went out—"Hey, get a load of this!"—and an audience gathered, a semicircle of naked, dripping bodies. The talk *about* him shifted to jeering *at* him. He tried to act as if he didn't hear them, but he could feel his face flushing. *Get through, get through, get out of here!*

He rinsed as well as he could, never turning away from the wall, then headed for the towel-off area, not meeting their eyes, trying to ignore their comments about his face, his body, his groin. But the arrows were landing with painful accuracy: *Ugly. Wimp. Gross. Little girl.*

He grabbed a towel off the cart and draped it around himself before he even started drying with it. Even that action brought lewd comments and another lesson: Once it begins, no action, no words, no change in behavior will turn it back. Once you're the target, *anything* you do will bring another arrow.

And so the arrows flew: two, then three, then more. Obscenities, insults, put-downs.

Along with his hurt, he felt a pitiful, helpless anger. He wanted to lash out, to tell them to stop, to defend himself, but he was all too aware of his body, just as they were. He could never match the strength of any one of them, much less the whole gang, and they were waiting, even wanting him to try.

Snap! Stinging, searing pain shot up from his groin like a jolt from an electric cattle prod.

"Oh," hollered a jock, "*good* one!"

Snap! He heard the sound again as a towel whipped past his backside, missing by a millimeter. A big lug with a hideous grin pulled his towel back for another try, then he jerked it toward the boy's body again, snapping it back hard, turning the moist end of the towel into a virtual whip. The edge of the towel struck between the boy's legs, stinging like a cat-o'-nine-tails.

He cried out in pain while they laughed. He raised a knee to protect his groin but lost his footing on the wet tile and tumbled to the floor, his hands skidding on the slimy, soapy residue. He struggled to his feet. A wet foot thumped into his back, and he careened toward a locker-room bench loaded with laughing naked bodies.

"Get off me, you fag!" Rough hands pushed him and he crunched into another body. "Get away, twerp!" They were angry with *him*. He was the Ping-Pong ball being batted about, and they were angry with *him!*

"Hey, squirt, you lookin' for trouble?"

"I think this kid wants a fight!"

He fled to the only square foot of floor that might be his own, the space in front of his locker. His body was throbbing, his bruises a combined chorus of pain.

And his soul . . . oh, his soul. He was choking back his tears, hurrying, fumbling to get his clothes from his locker, resolving to remain silent, desperately hoping no one would see him crying—but deep inside, his soul wailed in anguish, and there were no words or thoughts to heal it. Parental advice came to his mind, but it carried as much weight as a cookie fortune: "Just ignore them." Ignoring was only acting. It didn't stop the arrows from cutting through his heart. He even believed the taunts and stinging words. *Dear God, am I that ugly? Am I that weak and worthless?*

"Hey, nude boy! Hey, nature boy!" Now the teacher's assistant, just a few grades ahead of him, was getting in a few jabs. "Get the lead out. The bell's gonna ring in five minutes."

He got the lead out. Still wet, he threw on his clothes, missing one buttonhole in his shirt so that the shirt hung cockeyed on his back, but he didn't care. He grabbed his books out of the locker—

A hand slammed him against the locker, and his head bounced off the steel door. His books fell to the floor, the pages crinkling, his assignments spilling everywhere. He'd only begun the thought of picking them up when one of the jocks grabbed him around the neck, lifted him off the floor so his feet dangled, then dropped him on his books. He crumpled to the floor, gasping.

A whistle shrieked. It was Mr. M, angry as always. "Line up, line up!"

The T.A. yanked the boy to his feet. "C'mon, get in line!"

He gathered up his books, some of the pages wet, wrinkled, and grimy, and plugged an empty spot in the line.

One minute to go. He'd never felt such longing to be somewhere else. Somewhere in his memory—right now, a *dim* memory—was a kinder world than this, a place where he could find some measure of his lost dignity, the last broken tatters of his self-respect.

The bell rang. Could it be over? Could it finally be over?

Mr. M swung the door open. The lines started moving, a few boys at the front of the line darting off as though they were in a race for their lives.

"No running. WALK!" Mr. M growled.

The stream of bodies poured into the narrow hall, and in a moment he was hurrying away from that place, taking several last looks over his shoulder, checking for danger, thankful he could still turn his neck.

In the main hall, he passed the trophy case, where the glories of his high school were on display. Here were the school colors, pictures of the school mascot, the trophies, the ribbons, the news clippings, the victories—everything a kid should be proud of. His eyes flooded with tears. When he first came to this school, he looked in that trophy case, and, yes, he was proud. He was filled with an exhilarating joy and a sense of belonging. School spirit, that's what it was. He couldn't wait to buy a pennant to hang on the wall of his room.

But now, all he could do was shed tears and wonder, *How could a school like this*, my *school, have a place like* that? *Does anyone care? Does anyone even know?*

In his next class, he sat at his desk, his clothes still damp, his body still aching, unable to keep his mind on the teacher's lecture or his eyes on the text. The mocking faces and the derisive, searing comments kept playing and replaying in his mind, overpowering anything and everything else.

And from the blood pooling on the floor of his soul, in the loneliness of his hurt and anger, in the escape of a neutral location, little thoughts were firing off in his mind like forbidden firecrackers: *Oh, right, Mr. T.A., sir, Mr. Big Tough Guy, Mr. M in miniature. You wouldn't be so tough if Mr. M weren't around. And as for you, Superjock and Dumb Thug and Towel Turkey, if I were bigger, if I were stronger, if I could . . . if I could . . . oh, man, if only I could . . .*

But he was a Christian. He wasn't supposed to think such things, so he tried not to.

And he said nothing, and he did nothing, and when the day for gym class came around again . . . he went back. After all, the authorities in his life had made clear certain axioms: He had to be there. There was no choice.

January
12-13, 1951

Chapter Two

Snow, and more snow. Howling wind that shrieked through the cracks. Darkness beyond the headlights of the old car, and in the headlights, white on white on white: frost and ice on the windshield, the snowstorm swirling in the lights like a universe of frantic white flies; and somewhere out there, only sometimes visible, the road, hidden under packed snow, fallen snow, blowing snow.

The windshield wipers were pushing aside ragged arcs

of visibility, gathering and stacking the loose flakes but chattering ineffectively over the ice droplets encrusted on the glass. The windshield had the clarity of a shower door.

"Gene, we have to hurry," his pregnant wife urged, grasping her rotund belly as if holding it would lessen the pain. "They're getting close together." She stifled a whimper as another labor pain flashed through her body then said just audibly, "We're not going to make it."

"We're gonna make it, Joyce. We're gonna make it. Just hold on." With his sleeve he rubbed the condensation from the windshield of their eleven-year-old 1940 Ford. What was water came off. What was ice remained. What was breath became water that became ice just behind each sweep of his arm. *Grreshshunk. Grreshshunk. Grreshshunk*—the wipers kept working, but the blades were beating themselves to death on the ice. They wouldn't last the night. Gene's eyes on the road formed a direct link with his right foot on the accelerator, nursing as many miles per hour as the darkness, the snow, and the road would allow.

Gene was thankful they'd rehearsed this trip, due to a false alarm earlier in the week. Joyce had been sure she was going into labor, and they'd raced the thirty-five miles to Galt Hospital, in the town of Lethbridge, in

Alberta, Canada. The contractions eased by the time they got there, and the doctor sent them home again. "It's not time yet," he'd said. "Soon, but not yet. We'll be waiting for you when the time comes."

The time came less than an hour ago. They'd gone to bed early, partially to get warm under the blankets since the outside temperature had plummeted to minus thirty degrees. Gene fell right to sleep, but Joyce could only fidget in the dark until, right around 11:00 P.M., familiar pains wrung her body, then subsided, then seized her again within the next ten minutes. She lay flat on her back on the bed, trying to relax, breathing deeply. Was it time? Should she wait to be sure?

She waited, wide awake, listening to Gene snore as the winter wind rattled the windows. The contractions didn't subside as an hour passed. Over the next hour they became more regular, the pain more pronounced. By 1:00 A.M., Joyce was sure. She reached over in the darkness and nudged Gene awake.

"Gene, it's time."

"Huh, wha . . . time for what? Time! You mean it's *that* time?"

"Yes, I think it is."

They didn't have a telephone, so they couldn't call

ahead to let the doctor know they were coming. All they could do was go and hope someone at the hospital could contact the doctor once they arrived. Huddling together, they made a dash for the car, the vicious north winds pelting their faces with snow until they could climb in and slam the doors shut.

"Brrrr, turn the heater up high," Joyce begged as Gene turned the key, hoping the freezing winds hadn't caused the car's battery to go dead.

The engine groaned reluctantly. Gene turned the key again. *Errrrhhhrrrrr. Errr . . . Ummunnnhhh!* The car's engine roared to life.

He eased the car away from the parsonage of the quaint country church he pastored and headed across the rugged Canadian prairie, the snow-packed gravel roads vibrating Joyce's stomach as they traveled.

"Gene," she cried, "slow down or I'm going to have this baby right here in the car!"

"I thought you wanted to get there in a hurry."

"I do, but the pain is—OH! Hurry, hurry!"

Gene shook his head. Slow down, hurry up—what was he to do? He laid a hand on Joyce's stomach as he pressed the accelerator. "Lord, help us, please," he prayed quietly. Time was so precious, and there was so far to go. So far.

Their first stop was to drop off their little boy, a toddler, at the home of a minister friend. Then it was back into the car and back into the blizzard. Now the minutes seemed like hours, the arduous cadence of the windshield wipers incessantly reminding them of the ticking away of precious seconds, precious seconds, precious seconds. No other vehicles approached or followed them. They saw no lights from houses, stores, grain elevators, anything. A black, roiling nether world lay just beyond the window glass, and they dared not think about it. They dared not imagine how truly lonely, vast, and vicious the Canadian winter could be.

The road was full of potholes, and the car kept finding them, bouncing and bumping. Then came a jolt downward—Gene thought it was another pothole—but the front end of the car didn't bounce back up. Instead, the car lurched sideways and skidded. They could hear the shriek of metal grating against metal. Joyce screamed, bracing herself against the dashboard. Their bodies heaved forward and then violently backward as the Ford ground to a halt, the front end drooping.

"Are you okay?" Gene yelled loudly.

Joyce pushed herself back up in the seat. She put her hands under her bulging abdomen and pulled gently. "Yes,

I think so." She straightened her rumpled, heavy coat covering the baby. "I don't think we hit the dashboard."

Gene let his head drop backward on the top of the seat as he exhaled a sigh of relief. "Thank You, Lord."

"What happened?"

Nothing came to mind. "I don't know, but I better find out."

"Yes, *please*." Joyce winced as she felt another contraction grip her body.

Gene reached for his wool cap. "Stay right here. I'll see what we're looking at." He put on the cap and grabbed his wool scarf. "Make sure the car keeps running so the heater will work; give it some gas once in a while so it doesn't stall."

"You be careful."

"I will. Don't worry." He wrapped his scarf tightly around his neck, put on his gloves, and opened the car door. The bitter cold air, filled with icy flakes, poured into the car as if into a vacuum. He quickly stepped out into the snow, slamming the door behind him.

The Ford's headlights lit the area in front of the car, but it was difficult to see into the front wheel well. As Gene's eyes adjusted to the dimness, he stooped down, felt for the tire—and felt nothing. No tire, no wheel.

Only the lug nuts remained, still fastened to the brake drum. He squinted in the darkness, peering through the blowing snow, trying to trace any track the departing wheel might have left. It could have landed in a nearby ditch, but searching for it would be next to impossible.

The car had a spare, mounted on a wheel, of course, so that option made perfect sense. He could replace the lost wheel with the spare, just as if he were changing a flat tire. Tomorrow in the daylight, after Joyce and their new baby were comfortable in the hospital, he could return and maybe find his other tire.

The trunk lid groaned and snapped away the ice in its seams as Gene opened it. He groped, found the spare, then loosened the clamp and pulled it out. He let it bounce on the ice—Good! It still has air in it!—then rolled it to the front of the car where he leaned it against the fender to keep it out of the snow. Now for the tire jack. He shuffled back through the snow to the trunk.

He quickly found a tire iron, but his groping hand couldn't encounter a jack no matter where he searched.

Then it hit him, like a sledgehammer in the stomach: *I left the tire jack in the school bus!*

He'd been driving the school bus to make some extra income—pastors of small, rural churches often did that sort of thing—and he'd needed the jack aboard the bus last week. That's where it was, right where he'd left it. He sagged against the rear of the car, filled with frustration for such an oversight. His wife was in labor, their car was slouched forward on three wheels, it was thirty-two below, it was dark, and he had to replace a tire without a jack!

What to do, what to do? *Think!* He looked through the car window. Joyce had leaned back on the front seat, her eyes closed, no doubt confident that her loving husband could rectify whatever the trouble was and they'd soon be on their way to the hospital. No use in frightening her. Let her rest.

What to do? He prayed, "Oh, Lord, help us. There's nobody around for miles, and we're about to have a baby in the freezing cold. What can I do?"

Looking around for an answer, any answer, his eyes fell on a road sign just within the car's headlights, a yellow diamond with a bent black arrow advising of a left turn ahead. It was bolted to a four-inch-by-four-inch post. A long post. Eight feet of it was above the ground, and there had to be at least another two feet under the ground.

A lever.

He needed a fulcrum. He peered into the dark trunk and spied his old, metal toolbox. It was only about eighteen inches long, ten inches wide, and about twelve inches deep, but it was rugged and strong. He pulled the box from the trunk and set it next to the bumper of the car, his gloves sticking to the metal in the cold.

Now to get that post out of the ground. The storm and the snowplows had piled the snow waist-deep around it. Gene pushed his way through, and then he dropped to his knees and dug the snow away with his gloved hands. The ground beneath was hard and crystalline with ice. He attacked it with the tire iron, gouging and chipping, scooping up the loose chunks with his hands. He dug and dug, the knees of his pants soaking through, his eyes watering, his nose running, the frost forming on his eyebrows, sweat pouring down his face despite the bitter cold. *How deep does the highway department put these poles, anyhow?* He stood up and wrestled with the post. It wiggled!

Gene dropped to his knees again, digging faster, gouging harder, his breath turning to ice in the car's headlights. He stood and slammed into the post with his shoulder, so focused on the task and so cold, he barely noticed the resulting bruise. He went to the other side and rammed it the other way. He slammed into it a few more times, back and forth. More digging and gouging, then some shaking, pulling, heaving one direction then the other. It had to come out. It couldn't be much deeper. Got to keep—

The sign tipped over.

With a desperate heave, Gene pulled the signpost off the ground and dragged it over the snow to the front left side of the car. His toolbox, his fulcrum, was ready. He pushed the part of the post that had been in the ground under the car's bumper and positioned the center of the post on top of the metal toolbox. The road sign at the other end lay flat, about fifteen inches off the ground. With the lever and fulcrum in place, he shoved the spare tire up against the wheel well. If he could raise the car just enough, long enough . . . if he could get the wheel on the lugs quickly enough. *If.* He might only get one chance at this.

He tried the makeshift lever. He could make the car rock upward, lifting the axle and brake drum off the ground, but he couldn't lift it far enough to get the wheel on. He needed more weight on the road sign. Gene looked around in the darkness, hoping that he might find a few rocks that he could pile on the sign, or maybe a heavy log. No such luck.

There was only one thing to do. He looked through the window at his young wife. Ordinarily, she was a small, petite woman, but with the extra weight she had been carrying through the pregnancy, she could barely waddle from place to place. Gene breathed a silent prayer of thanks for Joyce's extra pounds. Her weight, combined with his effort, might be their only hope.

Gene opened the car door. "Joyce! I need your help!"

The cold air shocked her awake. "What do you want me to do?"

"I need you to get out of the car. Wrap up warm. And please don't make any sudden moves. Just very carefully slide out of the car. Here, take my hand. I'll help you."

Joyce reluctantly tightened her scarf around her neck, buttoned her coat, and put on her gloves. She moved her right leg toward the door, while Gene held both of her hands. Slowly, carefully, she slid her leg out and placed her foot awkwardly in the snow.

"You're doin' fine, Joyce. Just go slow. Take it easy. I've got a good hold on you, so don't worry; you won't fall."

Joyce struggled to pull herself toward the doorway, getting colder with every moment. Finally, her left foot pushed down into the snow, and she eased upward, Gene's strong hands and arms there to steady her. The moment she was standing, another contraction wracked her body, and she nearly tumbled over in pain. "Oh! Oh, Gene!"

Gene held her tightly until the spasm passed, and then he slowly released his grip. "You okay?"

"I'm fine." Joyce straightened as best she could. "What do you want me to do?"

"I want you to come over here and sit on this sign," Gene said, leading his pregnant wife by the hand toward the driver's side of the car. "Watch your step."

"Sit where? What are you talking about? Gene!"

"Right over here." Gene pointed to the road sign as he helped Joyce through the snow. "Careful now. All you have to do is sit on the sign and try to put as much weight on it as you can. We don't have a jack, but if you can bounce on the sign a bit, I think the car will come off the ground enough that I can get the spare tire on."

Joyce recognized her husband's incredible presence of mind and ingenuity in rigging the lever and fulcrum from the post and toolbox in the freezing cold. She didn't even bother to question whether it was dangerous for her or the baby to be bouncing on a road sign. She carefully stepped up to the sign, turned, and planted herself on it. Then, by pushing against the ground with her feet, she raised her end of the signpost for the first bounce. She relaxed her legs and let the sign sink beneath her.

"Don't bounce too hard!" Gene called, kneeling in

24

the snow next to the wheel well, waiting for the precise moment when the car raised enough to slide the tire on. "I don't want the post to snap." With a grunt, he shoved the tire closer.

The Ford inched off the ground, slightly at first, as the post caved in the top of the toolbox with a crunch. Another bounce, and the Ford creaked upward six more inches. They needed two more, if the lever could just hold long enough!

Gene worked feverishly, shoving the tire into the wheel well. "Keep going! Sit as close to the end as you dare!" He put his shoulder under the wheel well, ready to push up with the next bounce. "One more bounce!" The signpost was bowing on the ends. It wouldn't last much longer. "Once more, now! Bounce on it, *now!*"

As Joyce bounced on the edge of the sign, the car eased upward just far enough. Gene slammed the wheel onto the lugs and held it while the car came back down on the tire.

"Hallelujah!" he shouted, scrambling quickly to retrieve the lug nuts with his bare fingers. The cold bit into his skin, but he couldn't care less. He had to get that tire secure. He twirled on one lug nut, then another, then another. His fingers felt like tree trunks as he reached for the tire iron to cinch down the nuts. The cold iron stuck to his hands but he kept working until—

"Okay!" The tire was on, fit and snug.

Joyce was still sitting on the road sign like a child on the low end of a teetertotter. Gene bounded through the snow to help her off the sign before she slipped into the snow.

"We did it!" he cried as he wrapped his arms around her and helped her to her feet. "Are you all right?"

"I'm okay. Just freezing!"

He got her back in the car, closed her in against the cold, then he returned to that blessed, hardworking, God-sent road sign. Exhausted and nearly frozen, he mustered his strength, picked up the post, and lugged it back to where he'd found it, dropping it back in the hole. It was tilting a bit, but it was back on the job—not that many travelers might be along to see it anytime soon.

Gene hurried to the car and jumped in behind the steering wheel. He tried to squeeze his fingers around the wheel, but it took several minutes before the feeling returned to his fingers enough for him to drive. "Thank You, Lord," he said.

"Yes, indeed. Thank You, sweet Jesus," Joyce echoed. "And now, please help us get to the hospital."

Gene revved the engine that had continued running through the entire ordeal, and they were off again, Joyce's contractions growing more frequent and more intense with each mile. When they finally arrived at the hospital, it was approaching 3:00 A.M. on Saturday morning. Gene left the car in front of the emergency entrance and ran in to find a doctor, a nurse, anyone who could help him get Joyce into the delivery room. At that hour there was no doctor, but he found a few orderlies.

"Let's just get her inside to a delivery room," said one, "and then we'll proceed from there!"

"Here—please call our doctor." Gene handed a piece of paper with the doctor's name and phone number on it to one of the orderlies as a woman in a blue uniform whisked Joyce down the hall on a gurney. In those days, fathers were not permitted in the birthing room, so Gene was directed to a room where he was instructed to wait.

Meanwhile, the intern took Joyce to an empty delivery room and helped her get situated. A nurse came in and told her, "We haven't been able to reach your doctor by phone, but we'll keep trying. Just try to relax, and don't worry. We'll be right down the hall in the nursery. Ring this buzzer if you need anything."

"But I'm—"

"The important thing is that we don't want the baby to come too soon. Don't force anything. Give yourself time. That way when the doctor gets here, you'll be ready."

"I don't think it's going to be that long."

The nurse scowled. "Try to wait until the doctor gets here," she said curtly. Then she walked out of the room, closing the door behind her.

Joyce lay flat on the gurney for what seemed like hours, enduring the contractions, counting the minutes between them. The contractions were coming very quickly now, and they were much stronger. The baby would be born soon. She reached for the buzzer and pressed the button. She waited, trying to relax, gathering her strength for the impending delivery.

No nurse. She waited. And waited. She pressed the buzzer again. Still no nurse came through the door. The door was closed, and Joyce didn't dare try to get off the gurney to call for help. She squeezed the buzzer again—harder, holding it there. *Where are they?* She could feel the baby pressing against her. "Help!" she called out. "Somebody, please! Help me! The baby's coming!"

Joyce squeezed the buzzer again, alternately pressing and releasing it, pressing and releasing. Wherever the buzzer was ringing—if it was ringing—somebody was bound to notice. Finally, a nurse she'd never seen before—she turned out to be the head nurse from the floor *below*—came running into her room, took one look at her, and slapped an ether mask over Joyce's face. That was the last thing Joyce recalled. She still had not seen a doctor. She'd hardly even seen a nurse.

Sometime later—how much later, no one knows—the doctor finally arrived from his amblings somewhere out in the cosmos and got involved with the birth of the child. Because of the forced delay in delivery, the baby had shifted around to a near breech position.

"Forceps!" he called to the nurse. She slapped them into his hand, and he managed to clamp them around the baby's head. They had to reposition the baby to be born naturally. There was no time for a Cesarean section at this point. The baby needed to be born now . . . or never. They worked feverishly, pressing on the mother's abdomen, pulling on the forceps, repositioning, pressing, pulling. Finally, with one last yank, the baby was born.

But not without injury. At some point the forceps had slipped off the head and traumatized the right side of the neck just under the jaw. No matter. The little boy was badly bruised, but he was breathing and very much alive!

A short while later, the doctor stepped into the waiting room where Gene was pacing anxiously.

"Congratulations, Mr. Peretti. It's a boy."

Gene made it to the recovery room only moments after Joyce woke up. In her arms lay a baby boy, his eyes closed, his tiny body bundled in blankets. "Oh, Joyce!" Gene gushed through tears of joy. "Thank You, God! Thank You for this new life." He kissed Joyce lightly on the forehead and gazed lovingly at their child. "So, I guess we're naming him Frank Edward."

Joyce smiled. "Mm-hm." They'd already discussed what they would name the child once they knew its gender. They would name a boy after Joyce's brother Franklin and give him Gene's middle name. "Frank Edward."

"Hello, Frank! Nice to have you with us." Curiosity, and then concern, quelled his smile. He fingered the blanket away from the baby's neck. "What's this?"

"The doctor said it was nothing to worry about," Joyce replied, but her voice was troubled, unbelieving. She lifted the child and turned him gently. The baby's head just wouldn't lie naturally. The neck seemed strangely crooked. "Do you think something's wrong?"

Gene stroked the tiny head and said nothing.

"Gene?"

Their eyes met, and neither could hide what each was sure of.

Something was wrong with their child.

Complications

Chapter Three

I t's called *cystic hygroma*, defined by the medical
dictionary as "a lesion caused by a mass of dilated
lymphatics, due to the failure of the embryonic
lymphatics to connect with the venous system." It's a
birth defect that usually develops on the side of the
neck, so I suppose the role of the doctor's forceps in
delivering me is debatable. Whatever the case, the folks
at the hospital never got a clue—or never wanted one.

As was customary in 1951, Mom's doctor insisted that

she stay in the hospital for several days before he would discharge her, and those days became a disconcerting la-la land of denial on the part of the medical staff. My head still rested awkwardly, I wasn't eating much, and what little nourishment I could handle didn't stay with me long. Whenever Mom expressed her concerns to the doctor and nurses, they all pooh-poohed the problem. "Don't you worry, Mrs. Peretti. You're gonna have a big, strong boy there. Just like his dad."

Mom also asked about the small lump on the side of my neck.

"Oh, it's nothing," Mom's nurse assured her. "The doctor used forceps to help draw the baby out during birth, so it's probably just a little bruise. It will clear up in a matter of days, and your baby will be fine."

Well, they *were* the medical experts, weren't they? Mom and Dad accepted the assessment and took me home, fully expecting the lump to dissolve within a few days.

It didn't.

Instead, it grew larger . . . and larger. Within a month, the lump on my neck had swollen to the size of a baseball. I could barely swallow.

As God's providence—oh, so mysterious and so painful

at the time—would have it, Dad's ministry at the little church came to an end, and it was time to move on. Dad's folks, my grandparents, lived in Seattle, so we traveled there to live with them while Mom and Dad figured out the next direction for their life and family. Concerned that the lump on my throat was expanding, Mom took me to another doctor, to get a second opinion. This physician took one look at my neck and declared emphatically, "We need to get him to the hospital right away!"

My parents took me to Children's Orthopedic Hospital in Seattle, where the doctors quickly diagnosed my condition—and none too soon. Cystic hygroma can lead to obstruction of a person's breathing; it can cause nervous palsies, possible hemorrhaging, and infection, and I was showing signs of developing everything on the list. It was time to operate.

I was barely two months old when the doctors cut my neck open, trying to clean out a swollen mass that threatened to kill me!

They succeeded—mostly—and then kept me in the hospital for ten days to watch for possible complications. It must have been a long haul for a newborn. Mom recalls that when they finally placed me back in her arms to go home, I was a tiny "bag of bones," with a long scar and black sutures that made it appear as if my head had been nearly severed and then sewn back on.

"We've done all that we can," the doctors told my parents. "Just take him home and love him, and that will be the best medicine for him." Although the doctors informed Mom and Dad that a recurrence was possible and that cystic growth into surrounding tissues was unpredictable, they didn't expect any complications.

Mom and Dad got back to building their life. Dad went back to working at the luggage factory where he'd worked while attending Bible college, and we did all right. Thanks to the love of my folks and my older brother, Terry, I fattened up again just fine.

But then came complications the doctors didn't expect. As they'd said, cystic growth can be unpredictable, and the unpredictable happened. My tongue began to swell, and before long, it was hanging out of my mouth, oozing a fluid that turned to black scab when it contacted the air. I drooled constantly, leaving bloody, blackish residue around my mouth and chin, down the front of my clothes, and on my pillow. I was having trouble eating—imagine trying to swallow, even chew, without the help of your tongue!

I became a frequent and familiar patient at Children's

Orthopedic Hospital. The doctors feared cancer, but one elderly surgeon had seen my symptoms previously in another patient, a little girl, whose precious face had been hideously distorted due to her condition. The doctor guessed that the swelling in my tongue was the result of my earlier operation, during which the tumor had been removed. Some lymph glands had also been removed, so now my lymphatic system was secreting infection into my tongue.

It was going to be a tough problem to fix. With the tongue so enlarged, there was no way to shrink it down again except to *carve* it down. In the first of many operations on my tongue and mouth, the doctors literally cut a wedge of flesh from my tongue in an effort to keep it in my mouth.

Next problem: With my tongue carved down to a stump, it couldn't do the usual tasks a tongue is supposed to do. I could barely move it. Eating was difficult, speaking even more so. The surgeons operated again . . . and again, removing flesh below my tongue to free it up, then performing plastic surgery on my face around my jaw and chin. By the time I was four years old, I had endured seven rounds of surgery. I vaguely remember some of the later operations; I can still recall how unpleasant it felt, being tied to a hospital bed, being fed through tubes shoved down my nose, and having wooden sleeves holding my arms straight so I couldn't touch my face. I missed my family, I wanted to go home, and I wanted to sleep in real pajamas, not those goofy hospital gowns that are wide open in the back.

When at last the doctors allowed me to go home, the journey wasn't over. My tongue was still big and unwieldy, protruding from my mouth, and by now I was learning to talk that way. My speech was slurred, like Sylvester the Cat, and my tongue was still oozing fluid that caked on my lips and chin like dark chocolate—and sometimes sprayed on others if I pronounced a really strong *s*. I drew stares wherever we went. Mom, Dad, and my brother, Terry, were protective, but they couldn't possibly shield me from the natural revulsion most people expressed, knowingly or not, once they noticed the raw flesh and brown gunk in my mouth.

"Ooh, what's wrong with him?" the children, and too often the adults, would say. "Ooh, *yuck!*"

Can you figure God out? My folks did a lot of praying for me, as did the members of our church and all the extended family, gathering around me, laying hands on me, and praying that God would heal me.

Even Oral Roberts prayed for me. When I was around three years of age, the famous healing evangelist came to Seattle to conduct a crusade in a huge tent. Mom and Dad felt it was worth a try—you never know what God might do—so they took me to the service.

The tent was packed with the faithful, the hopeful, and the curious, and it was sweltering in there. Folks were fanning themselves with song sheets; you could hear the steady rustling, and the vast crowd looked like a forest of quaking aspens. But nobody left. They sat right where they were and listened in awe as Roberts preached an encouraging message about how Jesus healed everyone who came to Him and how we need to have faith.

Then came the climax, the moment the crowd anxiously anticipated: the prayer line. The evangelist invited those in the audience who needed a healing touch from God to move to the front of the tent so he could pray for each person specifically. Throngs of people went forward and formed the line along the front of the platform and around the side of the tent. This was it!

Mom and Dad pressed into the line, Dad carrying me in his arms, standing, then shuffling forward, then standing, then shuffling forward inch by inch while Reverend Roberts prayed for each person. Exciting things were happening up at the front of the line. Shouts of joy filled the air; some people were jumping, some cheering. The organ player was pounding out plenty of old-time praise songs for what God was doing. With each outburst, each victory, Mom and Dad's faith spiked upward.

Finally, it was our turn. While the organ played in the background, the evangelist leaned over so he could hear Dad whisper in his ear what the need was. Reverend Roberts didn't need a lot of description; he could see the problem for himself, and he appeared genuinely concerned, even *stymied*, by the sight of my dangling tongue. "Hand the boy up to me."

My dad has never been much of a weeper, but tears filled his eyes as he lifted me up and presented me to the healing evangelist. It was a moment of desperate hope, of clinging faith, of deep, earnest longing that somehow, somewhere in His inscrutable, mysterious nature, God would see fit to hear this prayer where other prayers had failed.

Standing on the platform in front of the massive crowd, Oral Roberts held me up in his arms and confessed, "I've never seen anything quite like this problem before." He prayed, and the crowd of believers prayed with him, that God would heal me. The organ played, the saints believed, and the cry went up to heaven, while the little slobbering kid in the middle of it all had no clue what the hubbub was about.

When Reverend Roberts handed me back to my father, I grabbed hold of Dad tightly, just glad to be back in his arms. Mom took a cloth diaper from her coat pocket—my ever-present drool rag—and dabbed the ooze from my mouth and tongue. My tongue was still running, raw, and grotesque as ever. Nothing had changed.

There was nothing more to do but go home.

My folks were sorely disappointed that I had not been healed instantly. Why hadn't God answered the many prayers offered in faith, believing God for a miracle? It's tough enough trying to figure God out, but especially when, to fulfill His plans, God seems a bit deaf. Making matters worse, of course, we usually don't get an immediate explanation.

Mom had been beating herself up emotionally and spiritually ever since my birth. She'd seen me suffering and had kept asking herself, "What did I do wrong?"

Satan was no help; he was always quick to tell her, "This is your fault." It was a lie and she knew it, but the thought stung her, clinging to her mind like a leech. At times, the punishing thoughts, the guilt, and the frustration hurt so badly she just wanted to take her baby and run away, to hide where nobody could find them and no eyes could stare at them anymore.

And now, it seemed that their last, best hope for my healing had proved disappointing. My disfigurement remained the same; the stares, snide comments, and Satan's devious accusations would all continue.

Dad kept a lot of his pain and frustration inside. That was just his way. But I still recall Mom telling me that the only time she'd ever seen him cry was when he was asking folks to pray for me.

Were the prayers doing any good?

Without a doubt! God has a knack for performing miracles that remain unseen only because of our shortsightedness. My folks knew that. Sure, it was painful and frustrating at the time, and the whole rotten mess could make them feel so helpless, but my folks knew that God heard their prayers, and applied every one of them to His divine purpose for Frank Peretti. *Of course* God heard the many prayers on my behalf . . .

and He answered them in His time, and in His way. The resulting healing process is still at work in my life to this day.

So Mom and Dad persevered in faith, trusting that God would eventually heal me in whichever manner He wanted. The surgeries continued, along with repeated visits to the doctor. Everything seemed to go so *sloooowly*, but my parents never gave up hope. They continued to believe God, and they trusted Him, one day at a time.

And really, when I consider my condition at the beginning, the Lord was very gracious to me. For a while, the doctors were concerned that my face would be misshapen or that my teeth would come in crooked because of the constant pressing of my tongue, but amazingly, my face maintained its normal structure, and my teeth came in straight. I could have done a lot worse. In researching cystic hygroma, I've found that other kids with the defect have had to bear a much greater burden of disfigurement.

My burden was limited to my ugly tongue and one side effect: my small stature. Apparently, my body had been so preoccupied with fighting off infection that it had to postpone growing. The doctors assured my folks that I'd catch up eventually. We would just have to be patient.

We got on with our lives, and life at home was normal enough. Dad changed jobs again and began his thirty-year career at the Boeing Company, so we moved into a house in south Seattle, on a hill just above Boeing Field. That was during the heyday of the B-52, and I want to tell you, those big birds were *loud* when they took off!

Mom and Dad loved my brother, Terry, and me, and we played together and got into fights over toys and got in and out of trouble like any kids would do. Our younger brother, Paul, came along, and Terry and I got jealous because Paul got to have Ivory soap in his bath and we didn't. Life was normal.

I was small and I talked funny, but that didn't matter at home. Mom and Dad always loved me and let me know that I was special, that I would grow up to be big and strong someday, and that the problem with my tongue would soon go away. I believed them, and, really, we did all right.

And then . . . I had to go to school.

Monsters on the Loose

Chapter Four

Come on, honey; it's time to go to school," I heard Mom's voice calling. "You are going to have so much fun. You'll get to color and play games and listen to stories. You'll love it!"

Mom checked my sweater to make sure I was dressed just right for my first day of kindergarten. My tongue still protruded from my mouth, and I had difficulty pronouncing many words, but I had developed my own way of saying words when my tongue refused to

cooperate. For the most part, I could communicate
fairly well.

Going to kindergarten was almost like being at home.
The teacher was kind and loving, and she never said a
word about my disfigurement. At first, most of the
children were kind, too, or maybe they were just as awed
by the school experience as I was, so I didn't receive
many snide remarks. As the year went on, however, the
teasing began.

Children can say the funniest things. They also can
say some of the cruelest things imaginable. Even at that
young age, the kids seemed compelled to remind me
about the scab-covered tongue hanging from my mouth.
By the end of my kindergarten year, I'd had quite
enough of school and didn't want to return.

When Mom dropped me off at school to begin first
grade, I decided not to stay. By now, I was extremely self-
conscious about my size and disfigurement, so as soon as
I saw our car disappear around the corner, I ran away
from school and headed back home. I was like a human
boomerang, returning to the person who sent me out.
Sometimes, I got home before Mom parked the car in
our garage!

"I don't wanna go to school!" I railed.

"Frank, honey, you have to go to school," Mom insisted.

"No, I'm not going!"

"Yes, you must."

I loved my mother dearly, and she loved me, even as she planted deeply in my mind the axioms of authority that would follow me for years: "You have to be there. You have no choice."

She herded me into the car and drove me back to school.

One morning, after I ran away from school again and Mom took me back, my teacher told her, "You just leave him to me. I'll handle him."

Mom peeked through the window of the door to the classroom while the teacher took me back inside and kindly but firmly sat me down at my desk. I burst out in tears and wailed wildly. The teacher remained nonplussed. She gave me some special assignments and told me, "Now, Frank, stop your crying. You're in school now. It's time to do your work like a big boy." The teacher arranged my work on the desk for me and gave me enough to keep me busy for a while. She checked on me regularly, and before long, I became interested in the work and forgot about the incessant teasing of the other children.

Until recess, when it started all over again.

The scenario was repeated throughout my elementary school years. On one occasion, Mom and Dad complained to the school principal about the teasing. The principal listened attentively and apparently passed the word on to some teachers, but no amount of adult supervision could prevent the arrows from piercing my heart on the playground, in physical education class, or in the school bathrooms, away from the watchful eyes of the teachers.

The only safe havens were at home and at church. The kids at church had known me most of my life and understood that something was wrong. They were good friends. They had heard some of the adults praying for my healing, and some of them had even prayed for me themselves.

One Sunday morning, when I was about seven years of age, I was sitting in church, trying to keep from squirming around as Dad led the song service. My tongue was throbbing. Intense pain began to flare around my throat. Before long, I felt as if a lump of meat was stuck in my throat and I could barely breathe.

We weren't supposed to talk in church. We weren't supposed to fidget or make noise. So, since I had to scream and cry, I did it while running out of the sanctuary.

Mom came running after me. "Frank! What's wrong?"

I clutched at my throat, choking, tears streaming from my eyes. The more I cried, the worse the pain got. Mom took one look at my neck and saw the swelling around my throat.

Mumps! A serious enough affliction for any child, but far worse for a child with cystic hygroma! Mom raced to a phone and called our doctor, who prescribed medication to reduce the fever and swelling.

The medication did the trick and I was able to breathe more easily, but getting any food past my doubly swollen tongue and badly constricted throat was another matter. Mom and Dad had to feed me through a straw for several weeks. My bout with the mumps served to notify them that I was probably going to need more surgery on my tongue and mouth.

And so it went. Life was painful at times because of sickness, the world was cruel at times because of taunts and teasing, and the laundry could get gruesome whenever my tongue decided to have another "eruption."

But I just have to brag about my mom and dad.

Along with the Lord, they were the solid rock under my feet and never neglected any chance to encourage my creativity. I became interested in drawing and cartooning, so they supplied me with paper, pencils, and art books. I wanted to build a twenty-foot model of the *Titanic* in the backyard, so Dad let me use his tools and scrap lumber—provided I put everything away when I was done. My brothers and I set out to build some airplanes in the garage, so Dad moved the cars out and let us have at it. We were going to build a foot-powered paddleboat as well, and got as far as stacking some old oil drums—flotation—on the back patio for several months. I came up with an idea for a gas-powered, one-man blimp, but that never got off the ground.

Most of our big projects never floated or flew. Usually, we'd go nuts on one project for a few weeks, then we'd tear it all apart so we could use the lumber and nails to fulfill the next big vision. Mom and Dad just watched to make sure we didn't hurt ourselves, made sure we put things away and got our homework done, and went with the flow. Dad gave us advice, let us use his tools, and granted us room in the garage, on the patio, or in the basement, for as long as it took. Never once did he tell

us it wasn't worth it or that we'd never succeed or that
our ideas were dumb.

I *did* succeed with many smaller projects more within
my reach, working wonders with the cardboard from
empty cereal boxes. I built a spaceship, a three-story
haunted house, a jet airliner, a whole fleet of Boeing
727s and KC-135s, the Space Needle, the Seattle
Coliseum, and the Century 21 monorail out of cereal
boxes and good old, dependable Elmer's glue—they
were *toy* size, of course. I even got my picture in the
paper, standing next to my cardboard Space Needle.
Guess who made that happen?

One Christmas, Mom and Dad surprised me with a
ventriloquist dummy named Jerry, and that little
woodenhead became my alter ego, bringing out the ham
in me. We entertained our family members and put on
shows, and Jerry even went to school with me a few
times to perform for my class. Jerry and I became pretty
close. He helped me come out of my shell, we won
ourselves some new respect from my classmates, and he
never had a problem with my looks or size.

I will have to say that, all things considered, kids
having a loving mom and dad has always been a great
idea.

But even Mom and Dad had to wonder about another buddy of mine who came later.

Zenarthex was my most memorable creation. He was more than eight feet tall, with a jaundiced complexion, blue and red blood vessels stark and visible under his parchment skin, and a long, flowing cape that blew in the wind. His arms needed a little work, and he had no hair on his head, but his jaw moved, and his eyes—big, round, and bloodshot—gave him a chilling gaze. We still had several parts of him lying around the lab, but Terry and I figured he was finished enough for a test run. We threw him together and told him to stand out on the corner near the Graham Street Grocery late at night.

The breeze that night kept his big cape moving, and the cold blue of the streetlight made him look downright eerie. I couldn't have been more pleased. We gave him a thumbs-up and a quick slap on the back, then we hid behind some parked cars to see what passing motorists might do.

For his first time out, Zenarthex handled the job quite well. He stood there boldly, as an approaching car's headlights illuminated his huge frame and hideous face, his expression never changing, his big eyes never blinking, his toothy grin always steady. Most of the cars just drove on by—after all, this was in the middle of Seattle where most folks had already seen everything—but one car slowed down, and another actually stopped for a second look before speeding away with a roar and a screech.

Cool!

After about a dozen cars, we were satisfied. Zenarthex had had a successful debut; he had even scared some people! What more could we ask for?

Besides, Zenie was getting nervous. "It's after curfew."

Mm, good point. Terry and I joined him on either side and helped him see his way home, taking him back to our lab in the basement of our house.

We had a great lab, full of jars, bottles (mostly empty canning jars and ketchup bottles with dyed water inside), and cool mad scientist gadgetry (a dead television, the insides from an old Philco tube radio, the chopper from a broken cider press). We'd crayoned a brick pattern on the concrete walls, hung some of Mom's nylon stockings from the ceiling to simulate stalactites, and provided Zenarthex with his own slab (a door lying on orange crates) and a super electrical heart zapper (an empty can of talcum powder fastened to a length of gooseneck conduit with duct tape). We thought it might have been cool to get a red light bulb for the ceiling or maybe one of those Christmas tree floodlights with a rotating, colored disk to add some mood to the place, but this was a low-budget operation.

Zenarthex was too tall to fit under the basement ceiling, so we had to take him apart and carry him inside in pieces. Our lanky, six-foot friend Glen was glad enough to get the stick and cloth framework off his shoulders. I'd used a lot of plaster in making Zenie's head, and Terry had used a lot of hardware to get his mouth to work, so Zenarthex was heavy. He looked great, though, lying on his slab, all put together again, staring at the ceiling with those big, Ping-Pong-ball eyes. A few more dollars from returned pop bottles, and we might just make that monster movie for which we'd built all this stuff.

Ah, monsters. My friends. My associates. My obsession. By now, I was just on the brink of thirteen. John F. Kennedy was dead, the Beatles had just invaded, skirts were short, and pants were tight. My younger brother, Paul, and I had expanded our territories to the point of war in our old room, so now he had his own room, and I had mine.

But I was not alone in my room, no sir. The

Frankenstein monster was there, both as a wall poster and as a plastic model on my desk. I had other plastic models, as well, each meticulously assembled and painted: Dracula, gesturing hypnotically; the Creature from the Black Lagoon, poised to scratch someone's face off; the Mummy, all wrapped up and rotten; the Phantom of the Opera, singing an aria with his mask in his hand; the Hunchback of Notre Dame, bleeding from a whipping; the Witch, stirring up a potion in her pot. I had posters of monsters, monster masks (Terry looked better than I did in the Frankenstein mask; he was taller), monster magazines, and monster comic books. I wrote stories and drew comics about monsters and mad scientists; I told the neighbor kids stories about dead bodies and spooks, and I made audio dramas on my folks' old reel-to-reel tape recorder about devious, monster-stitching, body-snatching scientists with silly foreign accents.

I never missed Saturday afternoons on Channel 11 or *Nightmare Theater* on Channel 7, unique cultural opportunities to view some of the worst sci-fi and horror flicks ever made, all sponsored by our local honest and upstanding used-car dealer who would never lie to us.

I got to know by name the finest Japanese monsters

ever to don a fake rubber suit and destroy toy cities in slow motion.

I marveled at the possibility of things coming from elsewhere: Martians all slimy and slithery; Venusians with tiny bodies and big brains; and hovering, whammy-eyed Brains with no bodies at all from some planet that starts with a Z.

I saw just about every plot idea that can be milked from atomic radiation gone amuck:

Things made *big* by atomic radiation: giant ants, giant grasshoppers, giant lizards, a giant praying mantis, an amazing, colossal man, a fifty-foot woman . . .

Things made *small* by atomic radiation, like the incredible shrinking man . . .

Things made *weird* by atomic radiation: three-eyed, four-armed atomic mutants, one-eyed cave dwellers, goofy underwater monsters that swam like people . . .

Things made *invisible* by atomic radiation, *invincible* by atomic radiation, *wicked* and *depraved* by atomic radiation.

I saw atomic radiation depopulate the world—except for the leading man and leading lady, who survived to start the human race all over again—several times.

My world was filled with scientists fooling around

with things best left alone while a younger, wiser
scientist tries to warn them not to, as the pretty girl—
always in love with the younger, wiser guy—gets carried
off by the monster while the scientists are busy arguing.

But through it all, my keenest interest was in the
monsters, those ugly, misunderstood, abused, captive
monsters who escaped from their cages, traps, and
laboratories; scared people; broke things; and got back at
the unfeeling people who abused them. The three-eyed,
four-armed atomic mutants may have been victims, but
they turned around and *made* victims.

The Frankenstein monster was tormented relentlessly
by Igor, Dr. Frankenstein's humpbacked assistant, but
the monster got even. The Creature from the Black
Lagoon was captured and imprisoned in a huge
aquarium, but he finally clawed his way out of there and
got some respect. King Kong was captured and put on
display, but he snapped his chains, escaped, grabbed the
girl, and had a real heyday in New York City, at least for
a while. The Mummy got a raw deal in his time, but
eventually, he got a chance to even things up in ours.
Dracula could give his victims the Eye and cut right to
the chase. Both the Phantom of the Opera and the
Hunchback of Notre Dame were scarred, ugly, and

misunderstood, but at least for one poignant, wishful, intense moment, they had the appreciation of the girl.

No wonder I kept those guys around. Somewhere in my head, planted there repeatedly over the years, was the notion that I was one of them—ugly, rejected, picked on, and somehow less worthy of membership in the world of normal kids. I was entering adolescence, that weird age when the size, shape, and appearance of your body mean everything, and everyone seemed to be growing except me. On the right side of my neck, a visible scar and a depression could be seen where once there had been a tumor. Because of the problem with my tongue, I spoke with an obvious lisp and often mangled words when my mind darted faster than my mouth could follow. I wore glasses and one of two favorite vests every day, and let's face it, if I wasn't a bona fide nerd, I sure came close. Girls? Hey, I couldn't have been better protected from temptation. Once I lamented to my mom, "I'm so ugly, nobody would ever want to marry me!"

So it was predictable that some of my classmates— all of them bigger and proud of it—would take special pleasure in making my life miserable. I was pushed, shoved, thrown, hit, insulted, badgered, manhandled, teased, and harassed, and just as any monster must get tired of everyone screaming at the first sight of him (Why can't they just skip that part for once and say hello?), I was tired of kids asking, "Ooh, what's wrong with your tongue?" before they'd even ask me my name. Increasingly, through the eyes of others, I saw myself as a monster.

But my monster friends had one significant advantage I admired and wished I had: Yes, they were trapped and mistreated, just like me, but they found a way out. They were scarred and ugly, just like me, but if anybody ever knocked their books out of their arms, shoved them in the halls, drew insulting pictures of them, or called them put-down names, you can bet ol' Frankenstein or Phantom or Hunchback could do something about it. They had power over their situation. They had control. People were afraid of them and not the other way around.

Maybe you can relate. Ever been there? Maybe you're there right now, in a situation in which someone is constantly stabbing you with words, kicking you with cruel acts, hurting you, and taking away your dignity. You wish you could do something about it, get out of that situation, but all around you are those invisible walls, those axioms of authority that hold you in: "Well, you have to be there. You have no choice. You have to go. You have to be in that situation. We can't change anything."

You have to go to that school, sit in that classroom, eat in that lunchroom, work at that particular job, endure the taunts of that particular group, or put up with that boss, supervisor, or coworker.

Maybe you're the one who lies awake at night dreading every morning because of the people waiting for you at school or work. They have a name for you— it's not your real name; it's the one they gave you, something that labels you as inferior, ugly, or stupid. And there are others whom you don't even know, who don't know you, who call you by that name because it's fun for them. They have never bothered to ask you what your real name is. It's their mission to take away your dignity. They spit on you, trip you, knock the books out of your arms, and stomp on your ankles from behind. It doesn't matter what you wear, they laugh at it. If you own something new, they steal it, spill on it, tear it, and destroy it.

There is no particular reason for the torment. Any reason that can possibly be found or contrived will do.

They pick on you because you're smaller, because you have a rare blood type, because you pick apples on your way home, you sing a particular song, you wear a particular sweater, you can't throw or catch a ball, you can't run fast, you don't have the right clothes, or simply because you're different.

And in physical education class, your oppressors have the perfect opportunity to harass you, because they're in close proximity, and all the activity is physical. It's a convenient time to take physical advantage of you because you're small or weak or maybe not so great an athlete. So they push you and shove you, throw you, kick you, and trip you.

And there's nothing you like better than taking a shower with that bunch, being naked before your enemies, laid bare for them to spot your most intimate physical secrets so they can laugh at you, spread the word about you, torment you. Strangely, it's similar to a child being molested by a family member in authority. Parents and teachers—just like the stepfather, the father, the older brother, the uncle, or the live-in boyfriend— insist it's okay. They make you do certain evil things, simply because they said so; they tell you there's nothing wrong with it, but all through the obeying and the yielding, something deep inside you is crying out, "This is wrong! This shouldn't be happening to me!"

Those to whom you look for love, shelter, and protection tell you to ignore your tormentors, just to stay away from them, but the authorities do nothing to stop those who are verbally, physically, or emotionally abusing you. What's a person to do?

Ignore them? Let's be honest: Ignoring is *acting*, and nothing more—acting as though the words or actions of your oppressors don't hurt. You hear the words, you feel the insults, and you bear the blows. You can act deaf and impervious to pain, but the stabs and the arrows pierce you anyway.

Just stay away from them? Don't you wish that you had a choice? Can you choose which lunchroom to sit in, which squad to line up in, which desk to sit at, which bus to ride home, or which direction to walk home?

Remember? In P.E., "everyone is required to take a shower!"

If you say anything about the bullying you endure, you're a snitch or a wimp, and you only compound the problem. At least, that seems to be the universal, unwritten code of conduct.

If you had a choice, you wouldn't be there, but you

don't have a choice. You are hemmed in by the rules and requirements of the adult world, the expectations placed upon you from birth. Of course, you obey, of course, you do what you're told, of course, you submit to authority and authority's axioms, and, yes, in many cases, that is as it should be.

When an authority tells you, "You have to go to school," you go. You get dressed, grab your books and your lunch, and go. When an authority reminds you that your boss has a right to badger you at work because he signs your paycheck, you swallow hard and, with a sense of resignation, go about your work as though the belittling behavior by the boss never occurred.

By their indifference to abuse, bullying, and harassment, parents, teachers, and employers send additional, subtle messages often written between the lines: You must also endure whatever comes with the package. It happens. Life is tough. Kids will be kids. We all went through it. It's part of growing up. It's a rite of passage. Get over it. It'll make you stronger. Suck it up, kid. Hey, you wanna work here, you don't make waves.

Hemmed in, and with few options, you go every day, and you get stabbed every day, and you bleed every day.

But wounds can fester. They can become infected, and then they can infect others.

And they can *change* you because you haven't merely cut your finger or bruised your knee. You've been wounded in your spirit, and that wound pierces deeply, painfully, sometimes even permanently. As Proverbs 18:14 says, "The spirit of a man will sustain him in sickness, but who can bear a broken spirit?" When tough times or injuries come, we must be able to draw upon a reservoir of hope, faith, and self-confidence that God has stored up inside us through the love and encouragement of friends and family. If enemies, through cunning and cruelty, have plundered that reservoir, what will sustain us then?

Won't God sustain us? Won't He give us the grace we need? Don't we find our hope and strength in Him? Won't He get us through?

Absolutely. I wouldn't be here today if God's presence and grace were not true and ultimately provable.

But that's the rub: To prove anything *ultimately* takes time and experience. You have to live it out for a while, sometimes a *long* while. A process is involved. Even now, in so many of our lives, there are issues to be resolved and wounds that have to be faced squarely, forgiven, and healed. Many of us adults have been carrying unhealed wounds since we were children.

At the time of this writing, I'm close to fifty years of age, but I still remember the names and can see the faces of those individuals who made my life a living hell, day after day after day, during my childhood. I remember their words, their taunts, their blows, their spittle, and their humiliations. As I review my life, I think of all the decisions I shied from, all the risks I dared not take, all the questions I never asked, all the relationships I didn't pursue, simply because I didn't want to be hurt again.

Moreover, I am haunted by the tragedy of Littleton, Colorado, on April 20, 1999. We've heard the many theories and pontifications on why two students, Eric Harris and Dylan Klebold, strode into Columbine High School and massacred their schoolmates and a teacher. I'm sure the theories about violence on television and movies, violent video and computer games, the availability of guns, and the unavailability of parents all have their legitimate place in the discussion. I don't pretend to know with certainty what was happening in the hearts and minds of those young killers, and yet . . .

I remember the thoughts I had, sitting alone in the

school library after D. H. picked me up by my neck or sitting alone on the street curb, eyes watering, after P. B. sprayed deodorant in my face. I remember what I wished I could do if only I had the strength, the skill in martial arts, or the advantage that a baseball bat might give me over the bullies who bludgeoned and batted me around verbally and physically.

Of course, my parents taught me never to fight. I was a Christian; I had a loving God to turn to when times got tough, and I had a biblical code of conduct that required a nonviolent solution. I knew the Savior, who taught us to turn the other cheek and forgive. So, instead of retaliation or confrontation, I sloughed off the wounds inflicted by my abusers and retreated to the solitude and safety of my room, where I identified with monsters and tried to get by.

But immersing oneself in make-believe stories about monsters isn't the only way to deal with the pain and humiliation of being devalued by other people.

Nowadays, kids are devising all sorts of ways to identify with those who feel trapped and put upon, and this new breed of monster will do almost anything for the power to change his situation and get even.

Instead of getting into monsters, a modern-day victim

of abuse can gravitate to violent video games, in which he can vent his pain and anger by blasting his enemies into atoms.

He can watch movies—so many movies!—in which the hero solves his situation by shooting everybody and blowing everything up.

He can live in a fantasy world, in which he's the guy with all the power and all the guns.

He and his cohort can make a video for a class project, in which they dress in dark trench coats, carry guns, and blow away all the jocks.

He can customize the bloody "shoot-'em-up" game "DOOM," creating two shooters instead of one, giving them extra weapons and unlimited ammunition, and programming the game so the people he encounters can't fight back.

He might identify with a historical monster: Adolf Hitler, a tyrant who had total life-or-death control over millions, who could scare and terrorize people, and who could solve all his problems with guns and bombs.

He can fill his mind with Nazi mythology, wear a black shirt with a swastika, speak German in the halls and on his Web pages, and talk about whom he hates and whom he'd like to kill.

He can vent his rage with threats and obscenities on the Internet. The rantings of the Columbine killers are terrifying:

. . . for those of you who happen to know me and know that I respect you, may peace be with you and don't be in my line of fire. For the rest of you, you all better hide in your houses because I'm coming for everyone soon, and I WILL be armed to the teeth and I WILL shoot to kill and I WILL KILL EVERYTHING!

. . . Dead people can't do many things, like argue, whine, . . . complain, narc, rat out, criticize, or even talk. So that's the only way to solve arguments with all you out there, I just kill. God, I can't wait till I can kill you people. I'll just go to some downtown area in some big city and blow up and shoot everything I can. Feel no remorse, no sense of shame. I will rig up explosives all over a town and detonate each one of them at will after I mow down a whole area full of you snotty, rich, high-strung, godlike-attitude-having worthless pieces of ____. I don't care if I live or die in the shoot-out. All I want to do is kill and injure as many of you as I can. . . .[1]

He can give in to the hate that grows out of his wounds and talk about a plan to attack his school so much, and for so long, that eventually, as James 1:14–15 warns, the thought becomes an act, and the act brings forth death.

Finally, on April 20, 1999, Hitler's 110th birthday, he can carry out his most gruesome fantasy. And what better place than the school, where everyone, from the parents and teachers on down, has all the power, and he doesn't? What better place than in the high-school cafeteria, where students once surrounded Eric and Dylan and squirted ketchup packets all over them, laughing at them and calling them faggots while teachers watched and did nothing?[2]

And he can leave behind an e-mailed suicide note to the police (allegedly written by Eric Harris):

> . . . Your children, who have ridiculed me, who have chosen not to accept me, who have treated me like I am not worth their time, are dead. THEY ARE _____ DEAD. Surely you will try to blame it on the clothes I wear, the music I listen to, or the way I choose to present myself—but no. Do not hide behind my choices. You need to face the fact that this comes as a

result of YOUR CHOICES. Parents and Teachers, YOU [fouled] UP. You have taught these kids to be gears and sheep. To think and act like those who came before them, to not accept what is different. YOU ARE IN THE WRONG. I may have taken their lives and my own—but it was your doing. Teachers, Parents, LET THIS MASSACRE BE ON YOUR SHOULDERS UNTIL THE DAY YOU DIE. . . .[3]

Everyone has his or her own theory. Here is mine: Simply put, I believe that what happened at Columbine was the result of *a wounded spirit.*

Although the authorship of the above suicide note is in question, as are many details surrounding that day, to me, in the overarching scheme of things, it doesn't really matter. Whoever wrote it pegged the problem. We now have in our society myriad young people and adults who have been deeply wounded by the demeaning words or actions of authority figures or peers.

It is no secret that kids on the fringes of the cool crowd of Columbine endured their share of taunts and abuse. They were called faggots, were bashed into lockers, and had rocks thrown at them. They were shoved, pelted with pop cans or cups of sticky soda, splattered with mashed potatoes and ketchup, even sideswiped by cars while they rode their bikes to or from school.

One anonymous teen spoke of waking on school days with a knot in his stomach and the dread of having to face more humiliation at school. He would avoid certain hallways and even make his way to classes outside the school building to escape being ridiculed or bashed against lockers.[4] He knew Harris and Klebold were being tormented as well, and he said, "I'm not saying what they did was OK, but I know what it's like to be cornered, pushed day after day. Tell people that we were harassed and that sometimes it was impossible to take. Tell people that . . . eventually, someone was going to snap."[5]

I know how that feels. Maybe you do too.

Why is it so important that we address the problem of bullying and other demeaning attitudes and behaviors in our society? Because one in four bullies will end up in the criminal correction system.[6] Because those who have been wounded often become those who *wound* others. Because we could be allowing the creation of more monsters—the kind you never see, never expect, until they snap and take desperate, violent measures. And all of us—those who have been wounded as well as those who wound others—need healing, forgiveness, and a new heart attitude toward our fellow human beings.

No longer can we hide our heads in the sand and pretend that atrocities such as Columbine don't happen in our backyard. No longer can we live in denial, pretending that abuse does not occur in our family, church, or workplace.

It's time for change.

Finding a Voice

Chapter Five

Long before I became a published author, I was a public speaker. I spoke at youth rallies, retreats, Bible camps, church banquets, you name it. I did Bible studies, lectured on Christian world-view, preached the gospel, told wacky stories, delivered sermons, and covered all manner of subjects—all, that is, except the subject of this book.

I guess it seemed just a little too esoteric, too narrow in scope. After all, to my knowledge, I had never heard

anyone stand before an audience and address the matter
of boys, girls, men, and women demeaning each other,
picking on other people needlessly, and treating each
other with abject disrespect. Nobody talked about it in a
public forum—not parents, teachers, preachers, or
college professors.

Sure, we've all heard the subject of bullying
mentioned once in a while, usually treated as an
unpleasant nuisance, a rite of passage that happens to
everyone, no big deal. But I'd never heard anyone
actually *preach* on it. I'd never heard anyone come out
and say that bullying is *wrong*. I had to wonder, *If no one
else considers it important enough to talk about, how can
I be sure any audience will think it important enough to
hear about?* Though it was a significant burden I had
harbored secretly for most of my life, I never seemed to
find the right reason, place, and time to talk about it.

But then came the Life on the Edge conference for
youth and their parents in Ontario, California, on
Saturday afternoon, May 22, 1999. Focus on the Family
sponsored the event, and I was scheduled to be one of
the speakers during that weekend. I'd done LOTE
conferences before and had some prepared messages in
my files already, but things changed after the killings at

Littleton. The more I read and heard about that whole tragedy, the more I felt a quaking and stirring in my spirit, as if God were saying, *Frank, here is your reason and your place, and yes, it's time to talk about it.*

You may have heard the talk broadcast on the *Focus on the Family* radio program. When I first delivered it in Ontario, I was almost afraid I'd flopped, that I had failed to get my message across to the audience. As I presented the speech, I was way outside my comfort zone and choked with emotion half the time, being completely vulnerable about my experience. I told no jokes. I did no humorous routines as I normally do. I simply stood on the platform and shared from my heart. Nervous, and with little confidence in my memory, I leaned over my notes, even reading aloud from them at times. I rarely strayed from the podium, gesturing and moving around as little as possible while I spoke. I agonized through every word of the talk.

The audience of fifty-five hundred teens and their parents were respectful and receptive; they even applauded at times, but, for the most part, they remained still, subdued, and strangely quiet during my presentation.

Afterward, I came to understand why. This wasn't a

talk an audience could enjoy, applaud, and then yak about as they left the auditorium. This was a deep digger, a grave opener that scraped off layers of dirt revealing issues that had been buried long ago but were not really dead. For many in the room, my message was a painful reminder of past hurts and a call for reflection. For others, it was the emotional equivalent of a dentist drilling through a live nerve.

It's not a light and simple matter to open up and admit you're still harboring wounds from your childhood or to admit that, when you were a kid, you were bullied or abused or that you were the bully in someone else's life, the *cause* of the hurt. It's difficult to admit that you are being bullied or that you *are* the bully right *now*.

Heavy stuff. No wonder the audience responded in self-conscious silence.

Following my speech, the first feedback I received was from the sound technicians backstage. Of all people! These guys were adults, professionals, employees of Focus on the Family. They appeared to have perfectly normal, grown-up exteriors, all decked out with their Life on the Edge T-shirts and walkie-talkies. Nobody would have guessed that they had lived for years with a wounded spirit, with memories of sorrow, abuse, and loneliness, of being pariahs at their schools, on the job, or in their families. But they hadn't forgotten what those wounds felt like, and now, having heard me broach the subject and admit that the faces of my oppressors still haunted my memories, these adults felt free to talk about the ghosts from their pasts.

Later, I sat down with a charming couple, a drama duo who presented some remarkable parables and skits during the conference. They too had a story to tell about demeaning experiences in their pasts, and the similarities were disturbing and comforting; disturbing because the problem is so universal, but comforting because we could share so freely from a common experience.

After I got back home, I heard from the organizers of the event. No, I hadn't flopped as I had feared. Actually, I'd hit a nerve.

Dr. James Dobson heard a tape of my talk while exercising on the treadmill one morning, and it touched him so deeply he took his wife, Shirley, out for a drive that evening, and they listened to the tape again in the car. They agreed they had to share it with the *Focus on the Family* radio audience.

The opening words of the broadcast are worth

recounting. First came the telephone voice of an anonymous woman: "I was one of those kids who at one time in my life was mean to everybody else. I'm sorry . . . I'm sorry from the bottom of my heart. Please forgive me and forgive everybody else, because nobody deserves all that."

Then Mike Trout, Dr. Dobson's radio cohost, gave a warm and evocative introduction: "Did you ever pick on someone? Tease him or her for whatever reason? Well, of course, you did. Unfortunately, it's an event that happens far too often, and I'd go as far as to say you remember at least one occasion when you were made fun of too. Those memories are etched in our brains, and each occasion, each offense is an ingredient in the recipe that has come together over the years to create who we are today."

The recording of my talk followed, and I don't know what sort of response Focus on the Family anticipated, but *I* had no idea how vast an audience would identify with those words. After the talk was broadcast in October 1999, Focus on the Family received 3,375 telephone calls. When the same program was rebroadcast in December 1999, Focus received 1,264 calls. At least 316 callers requested tapes after the first broadcast and 1,117 callers requested tapes following the rebroadcast. The folks at Focus informed my publisher that these numbers are much higher than the usual response to a broadcast. Ordinarily, a response by one thousand callers is considered good; two thousand callers is beyond the best expectations. When *three thousand* calls come in, they know they've touched a nerve.

Now, I'm a writer with a name and an audience, so I wrote this book, but I realize that my story is nothing exceptional, that the wounds inflicted on me are marginal compared to those who have suffered severe child abuse, spousal abuse, verbal, sexual, or emotional abuse. My pain pales in comparison to that endured by the brave men and women who survived Hitler's concentration camps. When I think about the victims and families involved in the senseless murders of those who died in Littleton, Colorado, or the students who were shot to death in Paducah, Kentucky, or the tortures that many people have overcome in their personal lives, I'm embarrassed even to mention the bullying I experienced.

But we do have an issue here, don't we? I'm only one small voice in a sea of voices, and our issue is more than just a simple case of teasing. While we can all accept that bullying and abuse betray a lack or loss of respect for other human beings, there is a deeper issue: the devaluing of human life; and that in turn indicates a lack or loss of respect for the Giver of human life and dignity, God Himself. The message a bully sends is a mockery of God's handiwork, a lie that slanders God's nature and negates His love for us.

This could be important, don't you think?

Consider, for example, how such behavior can distort our view of God. In their book *The Sacred Romance*, authors Brent Curtis and John Eldredge describe the awful feelings of doubt and despair following the piercing of our heart by an offender's "arrow":

> The terror we enter and the seeming lack of rescue from it leave us with a deeply imprinted question about God that we hid in our heart, sometimes not allowing the light of day to touch it for years, even deep into our spiritual journey. We cover the question with rationalizations that let him off the hook and allow us to still believe, but our beliefs rest on foundations that move and quake under us. It is easy to reason that Jimmy and those sixth graders were just bad; you know, "not raised in very good homes." And of course, our

rationalizations do bear a modicum of truth that keeps us from dealing with the question lodged deep in our heart, hidden from our conscious mind: "Do you care for me, God?"[1]

Curtis and Eldredge go on to trace some of our misgivings about God to our childhood experiences, including the infliction of wounds by others. See if you can relate to any of these: "Parents who were emotionally absent; bedtimes without words or hugs; ears that were too big and noses that were too small; others chosen for playground games while we were not; and prayers about all these things seemingly met with silence."[2]

Ever been there? I'm beginning to find out that many people can strongly relate to these issues, more than we've ever imagined. It brings an interesting, television-like image to my mind: I see myself walking along in the center of a vast room, sort of like those all-white, cornerless sound stages you see in a television studio. For a moment, I think I'm the only one with a story to tell about childhood wounds that still hurt, but then, from one side, a sound technician comes along, an amicable guy wearing a Life on the

Edge T-shirt, carrying a walkie-talkie. He was the pariah of his class. He knows what I'm talking about. So we walk together.

Then comes a stage technician for Life on the Edge. And then the drama team that performed, and then a lady, a friend and listener of *Focus on the Family* who could hardly listen to the broadcast because it reminded her of the deeply buried pain from her past.

Then more people walk in from the sides and seemingly pop up out of nowhere, all shapes, all sizes, and all walks of life:

I see a columnist for a major Midwestern newspaper who once interviewed me. He's in his sixties now, and he has polio, so he walks with the aid of crutches. He's needed the crutches most of his life, but he's used to that. What really pains him are the wounds he can still feel, delivered by the kids who taunted him when he was a child.

Ah, here's the middle-aged woman who refuses to sing, even though she has a perfectly good voice and plenty of latent talent. She can remember the very day, during music appreciation class in the sixth grade, when she stopped singing. The other kids laughed at her and told her she sounded like a bird. Humiliated, she closed her mouth and has never opened it again to sing.

Here comes a beautiful, well-known screen actress. Nobody would guess that she had to wear a body cast for four years during her childhood. She was treated so cruelly by her classmates that she dropped out of school in the tenth grade and spent her teenage years as a loner, often hiding away in her bedroom with the door shut. Years later, after she had established a relationship with Jesus Christ, she was finally able to accept herself and to forgive those who had hurt her.

Please don't stare at that young man who is so excited about counting, "One . . . two, three . . . four, five, six, seven, eh-aa . . . eight . . . nine, TEN!" For him, this simple act is a major accomplishment, the opening of an immense door in his life. His father always told him he was so stupid he'd never be able to count to ten.

And along comes Shawn, the boy with the stutter and the harelip. He gave up learning to read because his schoolmates laughed and mimicked his attempts. He's thirty-seven now, and he still can't read.

"Hi, Joseph! Good to see you." Joseph has one leg that is shorter than the other, severely impairing his ability to run. He might have done well at any sport that didn't require him to run fast, but his gym teacher never told him that; the drill-sergeant-style teacher simply knocked points off Joseph's grade and mocked him, calling him "Slow Susie." Joseph didn't bother with any kind of physical fitness until well into his forties.

Meet Linda. She was excited about attending college until the very first day of classes, when a couple of senior girls insulted and belittled her for no reason other than the fact that she was a freshman. The upperclassmen didn't know her; they didn't even ask her name. Linda had been stung and hurt enough, all through junior and senior high school. She was not about to subject herself to that sort of treatment all over again. She walked off the campus and never returned, and, to this day, she's never obtained the college education she once dreamed of.

I look around at the growing crowd. Some people in our group are overweight. Some are small and weak. Some have physical deformities, cerebral palsy, or Down syndrome, or scars from burns. Others are Asian, African, Native American, racially mixed. It's not too hard to guess what their stories might be.

Others are more of a mystery. They look so normal, so "together," so everyday: One's a landscaper, another is an electrician, and over there is a mailman, and now I see a wife and mother, and next to her, a minister. You can't guess their stories. You're even surprised to learn they're carrying the same sort of wounds as you.

There's an important lesson in that: The wounded spirit is borne by many, yet it often can't be seen. It can be a burden heavy enough to bend and warp the course of our lives, but it's buried deeply, hidden in a secret place, and we've been afraid to talk about it.

Until now. I never thought I'd be some kind of Pied Piper, but suddenly, all these people who recognize the validity of what I'm saying are coming out of the woodwork. Some are still carrying deep wounds from long ago; some are enduring fresh wounds each day. As in the case of other secret scars, those individuals who have suffered a wounded spirit often suffer in silence, unwilling to talk about it.

But maybe it's getting to be *that time*.

Our society, and especially the Christian community, has been slow to discuss many sensitive subjects. Not too many years ago, domestic violence was something we only whispered about across the back fence: "Have you seen Lois this morning? She's all black and blue. Guess he's beating her again, poor thing." We gossiped about it, but beyond that, we felt it was none of our business. After all, those things didn't happen in our families, and certainly not in our church!

Similarly, just a few years ago, child abuse was something we suspected (and sometimes we were dead certain of it), but we hesitated to say anything. We weren't sure what to do. Besides, surely Christians would never be guilty of such a heinous crime. Sadly, we now know better, that such offenses happen in Christian homes almost in the exact same percentages as those of nonbelievers.

During my childhood in the 1950s and 1960s, the black man in some parts of the country was expected to "know his place," and we were comfortable with that. We were extremely uncomfortable talking about racism or attempting to change it. "Let them have their own baseball teams. Let them worship in their own churches. Not in my backyard."

So what about *this* problem? We call it by many names: Abuse. Teasing. Taunting. Harassment. Bullying. Until now, we've been strangely quiet about it. It happens, we say. We all go through it. All the kids do it.

It's part of life. It's no big deal. It happened when we were kids.

Is it wrong?

Let me ask again, *Is it wrong?*

Consider your answer carefully. If the answer is yes, that immediately raises another question: Then why do we allow it? Why do parents, teachers, teacher's assistants, fellow students, friends at school and church, coworkers, extended family members, and others see it happening, hear it happening, and know it's happening but fail to take it seriously? If devaluing human life—and thereby mocking God's creation—is wrong, why do so many do so little to stop it? Worse yet, why do so many participate as part of the problem?

Surely Mr. M was aware of what his students—and his teacher's assistants—were doing to that poor little kid in the shower. Surely the teachers and staff at Columbine—or any school for that matter—could hear the sounds of bodies hitting lockers, can see the ketchup stains all over some students' clothing, can hear the laughter of the bullies and the cries of the victims. Surely the bus drivers know when a gang of losers descends on one helpless kid, knocking his books all over the street at the bus stop. Surely the teachers notice when a child comes into class with his shirt torn, his shoes missing, and his clothing soiled. Most certainly, the kids know what's happening; they're a part of it. They face the bullying, badgering, and other such treatment almost every day in school; they're immersed in it. Why don't they attempt to put a stop to it, to refrain from such behavior themselves, and to confront it in their friends?

What about the parents of children who are being bullied? Do they have no options? Do they have no voice? Must they sit by in silence when they know their child is near vomiting from stress before leaving for school each morning? Or are they even aware of the problem?

But we're not just talking about school.

Even grownups have to put up with it. Sometimes it creeps into a marriage or into other family relationships. We might experience it at the hands of an overbearing minister, board member, policeman, or coach. Many people endure it in the workplace, sometimes even in businesses ostensibly run according to Christian principles and values.

Do we address it as something wrong that should not

be done, or do we just go on pretending we don't hear it, don't see it?

What about you? Are you being wounded senselessly, mercilessly, needlessly, by someone stronger than you, more powerful than you, someone who has leverage over you in some inexplicable, yet very real way?

Or are you the person who is perpetrating such despicable acts, either overtly or secretly?

It's time to talk about it, friend. It's time for a change.

Let me restate what I said earlier: The message a bully sends is a mockery of God's handiwork, a lie that slanders God's nature and negates His love for us.

Or do we really care about God?

As you can well expect, I will argue that a right attitude toward God will bring a right attitude toward our fellowman. As we have all seen clearly demonstrated, when God is removed from our thoughts, our lives, our schools, our society, any evil is possible, for we have no ultimate argument against it. Whether on an international scale, in your own neighborhood, or in your own family, the results are the same: People are no longer intrinsically precious, so it's easy to find petty reasons to mistreat the weak, the less intelligent, the less affluent, the physically disfigured, or those who, for whatever arbitrary reason, don't measure up.

In the next chapter, I'll share a parable with you that illustrates the absolute necessity for the inclusion of God in our thinking, our families, our world. If we really want to bring about change, this is where the change must begin.

The Playground Parable

Chapter Six

It was the daddy of all playgrounds, stretching out acre upon acre and filled with laughing, ebullient, playing children. Boys and girls were running, chasing, and screaming playfully. Jump ropes were spinning as little girls chanted rhythmical rhymes; baseballs arced through the air, glove to hand, hand to glove, ball to glove, glove to ground. From the paved basketball and Four Squares area came the constant *boing, boing, boing* of big red, inflated playground balls bouncing from one child to another.

This was a happy place—usually. The kids played well together and followed the playground rules—most of the time. Sometimes a quarrel broke out, occasionally even an actual fight, but these skirmishes were quickly resolved. All in all, the playground was a wonderful, fun-filled, safe environment for kids to enjoy.

The playground rules, clearly posted on a big wooden sign beside the entrance, helped to provide every recess with the desired peace, order, and domestic tranquillity. The rules were clear enough for any eight- or nine-year-old to understand:

NO HITTING.
NO PUSHING OR SHOVING.
NO FIGHTING.
SHARE THE EQUIPMENT.
TAKE TURNS.
NO SPITTING ON THE GIRLS.
NO CHASING THE BOYS.

The playground rules were sacred, omnipresent, and inscribed on every heart and mind; there was hardly a child there who hadn't had cause to appeal to those standards at one time or another.

For instance, when Jordan Smith first arrived on the

playground, he brought with him the assumption that once the baseball was in his hand, he had sovereign control over it in perpetuity. His would-be teammates tried to explain to him that unless he relinquished possession of the baseball from time to time, there would be no baseball game. Reason alone would not change his mind. Appealing to the playground rules finally did.

Clyde Saunders always seemed to have extra saliva in his mouth and apparently felt compelled to put it somewhere else. Rachel Parks was the nearest available depository, and he was happy to share with her out of his abundance, until she appealed to the playground rules, and he was required to swallow.

Ah, the playground rules—steadfast and sure, a shelter for the oppressed, the defender of the weak, the guarantor of social stability.

Of course, we cannot overlook the importance of Mrs. Kravitz, the teacher on playground duty. Mrs. Kravitz represented the authority that put up those rules in the first place. Without her presence, the playground rules would have been nothing more than words painted on a board. She was sharp-eyed and elephant-eared, always ready to help in time of trouble but also ready to deal with troublemakers. She had a stern expression for that purpose, as well as a whistle, a clipboard, and a stack of pink slips that could mean a visit to the vice principal.

Some of the kids appreciated her presence on the playground, and, naturally, some of the kids preferred she not be there. The former felt secure; the latter felt imposed upon. But like it or not, the playground was reasonably safe and orderly, because Mrs. Kravitz and the playground rules kept it that way.

Then one day, something was different on the playground. It took a while for the kids to notice, but eventually they realized that Mrs. Kravitz was nowhere to be found. Some were glad, of course. "Good riddance!" they said. But some were concerned and asked the other teachers where Mrs. Kravitz had gone.

"Well," said the teachers, "we've decided there is no authority, and you kids are inherently good and able to decide for yourselves the right thing to do. You have the capacity within yourselves to solve all your own problems and make this a better playground. You don't need Mrs. Kravitz."

"But what about the playground rules?" they asked.

"You can decide for yourselves if the playground rules are right for you. It's really not our place to say that any one set of rules is better than another."

And so the kids were left to their own wills and feelings and the whims of their own hearts.

For a time, the playground rules still held sway in their minds. The rules worked well enough in the past; they continued to bring stability in the days that followed.

But then, one day, Clyde Saunders stopped to consider the excess saliva in his mouth and whether or not he should swallow. "It's my mouth and my spit," he reasoned to himself. "I don't see what business anyone else has telling me how to get rid of it." Whereupon, he fired off a huge, viscid, undulating glob that hit Rachel Parks right in the eye.

Rachel was beside herself. She felt violated, betrayed, insulted, and infringed upon—not to mention wet and gross. "Clyde! You aren't supposed to do that!"

"Oh, yeah?" he responded. "Who says?"

She promptly took him over to the old sign displaying the playground rules.

"See here?" she said, pointing. "The rules say, 'No spitting on the girls.'"

"Well, I can choose to live by those rules or not."

"But you *hurt* me and you *know* it!"

"That depends on your definition of *hurt* and your definition of *knowledge*."

Not long after this, the baseball game came to a screeching halt when Jordan Smith caught a pop-up fly and abruptly walked off with the baseball.

"Hey," the others shouted, running after him, "that's our ball!"

"It's mine now," he replied.

"But you have to share!"

"Oh, yeah? Who says?"

They pointed to the rules. "It says, 'Share the equipment.'"

Jordan was unmoved. "You really *believe* that old sign? Come on, we don't need those rules. We have Reason to show us the way."

So they tried reasoning with him. After all, in the absence of authority, Mrs. Kravitz, and the playground rules, Reason alone should suffice.

"Well," he responded, "A: I want the ball; B: I don't want you to have it; and, therefore, C: You aren't going to get it!"

The other boys were stymied—except for those who weren't afraid of a little roughness. The rules didn't apply anymore, and Reason wasn't giving them justice, so . . . they ganged up on Jordan, knocked him to the ground, and got the baseball back.

Following Jordan's line of reasoning, Sally and Jennifer promptly took possession of a jump rope. The girls from whom they'd taken it tried to be open-minded and tolerant, but they still couldn't help feeling cheated somehow. "We think you should share," they said.

Sally rolled her eyes as Jennifer responded, "We think you should stop trying to impose your narrow-minded, middle-class morality on us."

"But remember the rules?"

Sally and Jennifer laughed mockingly in the other girls' faces. "We've evolved beyond the rules and attained a higher perception: We think the jump rope is ours. We think we're entitled to it. Therefore, the jump rope is ours."

This new way of thinking caught on. The children had no need of authority or Mrs. Kravitz anymore. Each child was his or her own authority. As for the rules, although the standards on the old sign beside the playground never changed, the rules became increasingly offensive. The children finally tore down the sign and threatened to kick and punch any kid who tried to put it back up.

So the playground was all theirs, and all the kids lived and behaved according to what felt right to them.

When the first real fight broke out and Tracy Sorenson beat the living tar out of Stevie Boland, the kids watched and debated what may have caused such a fight, but none of them could say it was anybody's fault. Nor did anyone say that it was wrong.

Since nothing was wrong or anybody's fault, every kid soon felt entitled to have or do anything, by any means. Since there were no rules and reasoning was inconvenient, the kids resorted to hitting, shoving, fighting, spitting, and chasing. The jump ropes, balls, bats, and other playground equipment became plunder to be captured, always going to the strongest kid or the biggest gang. Sharing came only with a price, and as for taking turns, the next turn always went to the toughest kid.

The playground fell into chaos. The big rubber balls didn't go *boing, boing, boing* anymore, and there were no more baseball games—no one wanted to play by the rules, and most denied there were any rules at all, so no one played.

A few, unwritten rules did crop up eventually, dictated by the toughest, meanest, strongest kids and very easy to demonstrate: Might Makes Right. Survival of the Fittest. Natural Selection.

Jordan Smith liked those rules because he was tough.

Unfortunately for Jordan, Tracy Sorenson was tougher. He beat the living tar out of Jordan Smith and established his reputation as the toughest, meanest, strongest kid on the playground.

Now it was forbidden to speak of the old authority the children had once known, and the memory of Mrs.

Kravitz quickly faded. The playground rules were gone, not only from the old wooden sign, but also from the minds and hearts of the children.

Tracy's will was now law. He controlled all the bats, balls, and jump ropes, and he decided who could play with them and when. He had a gang of tough boys and girls around him who enforced his will upon all the others through sheer brutality. There were no rules except his.

There was no longer any fun either.

The playground parable illustrates a familiar, historical pattern that is really no more complicated than the downward spiral we just traced on the playground. When we consider Stalin's Russia, Hitler's Germany, or the killing fields of Cambodia under Pol Pot, we see clear examples of what happens when man cuts away his moorings in God. At first, he thinks he is free, but then he realizes he is actually adrift, without a moral compass, in dangerous waters, where only the big fish win.

And the big fish can be horrendously mean to all the little fish when they have no absolute authority to whom they are accountable.

The Scripture records numerous times in the history of God's people when the majority of the population rejected God's revealed Word to them, and hence, God's authority. In describing one such period, one of the saddest, most poignant refrains in the Bible states flatly, "In those days there was no king in Israel; everyone did what was right in his own eyes" (Judg. 21:25 NASB). While at first glance that seems to imply that the Hebrew people enjoyed enormous freedom and autonomy, the exact opposite was true. The Book of Judges records a time of rampant immorality and chaos, with horrendous crimes against humanity. Predictably, the people fell into bondage to one tyrant after another, and God had to raise up a series of judges to deliver them.

In America, we haven't fallen under the heel of a ruthless dictator—at least, not yet. But we might ask ourselves: What point in the playground parable describes where we are today as a society? Here's a sobering hint, excerpted from the Eric Harris autopsy report:

HISTORY: This is the case of an 18-year-old, white male who was the alleged victim of a self-inflicted gunshot wound to the head that occurred in the Columbine High School library on 04/20/99. No other history is available at the time of autopsy.

EXTERNAL EXAMINATION: The body is clothed in a bloodstained white T-shirt with the inscription "Natural Selection" on the front. . . .

On his Web page, Eric Harris listed many things he hated, but Darwin's theory of evolution, particularly his suggestion of natural selection, stood in stark contrast. Harris's words are the haunting result of a playground in chaos:

YOU KNOW WHAT I LOVE???
Natural SELECTION! . . . it's the best thing that ever happened to the Earth. Getting rid of all the stupid and weak organisms . . . but it's all natural! YES![1]

When we pause to ponder what Eric Harris was wearing on the day he helped shoot to death thirteen people, we are well on our way to explaining why it happened.

Highly respected author and theologian Ravi Zacharias offered a profound insight in the days following the Littleton tragedy:

When we have told our young people today that Naturalism is true—we have evolved from nothing more than some primordial slime; when we have told them objective moral values do not exist—you decide what is right and wrong for you; when we have told our young people that there is no ultimate designer; when we have told our young people that there is no ultimate destiny;

when we have told them that man is the measure of all
things, that there is no transcendent basis on which to
find out what life is about and what life's goal is, why
then are we surprised when we see the hell that is
unleashed by that kind of philosophy?[2]

Ravi is right! I wish every teacher who indoctrinates
his or her students with Darwinian evolution, pawning
off unproven theories as fact, could be shown Eric's
bloodstained T-shirt. Remember the old movie *Inherit
the Wind*, in which Christians were portrayed as bigoted
nincompoops for opposing the theories of evolution? I
wonder if the makers of that movie (and a host of films
similar to it) might change their minds if they were
called upon to clean up the bloody mess in the
Columbine High School library. Oh, we've inherited
the wind, all right—and a lot more.

It's all perfectly logical: If evolution is true, then there
is no God. If there is no God, then there is no fixed,
external source of truth and morality. If there is no fixed,
external source of truth and morality, then truth and
morality are left up to the individual. If the individual
judges that killing all the "stupid and weak organisms" in
his life is justified and right, then by what basis can we

question his judgment? He's only following the moral compass evolution provides.

If all this sounds a bit boring, too pedantic, or too philosophical for you, keep in mind that the end result is extremely personal and practical. It touches nearly every part of your life, from what is being taught in your high-school and college classrooms, to what you hear in pop music, to what you see on television and in the movies, to what is being espoused by supporters of homosexual lifestyles, abortion, euthanasia, and assisted suicide, to radical, anti-Christian political movements, to neo-Nazi skinheads, and more.

Why? Because Mrs. Kravitz is barred from the playground. The rules have been abandoned and, in too many cases, jettisoned from the public square completely. In their absence, we are left to the dictates of our own hearts, and as Jeremiah 17:9 warns us and history has proved, "The heart is deceitful above all things, and desperately wicked."

Given all this, the question is not, Why did the tragedy at Columbine happen? but rather, Why *shouldn't* it have happened?

Why shouldn't kids taunt, tease, and torment each other? Why shouldn't bosses make unreasonable demands of their employees and then publicly berate them when the goals are not met? Why shouldn't a husband blacken his wife's eye as a reminder that he is the one in control? Why shouldn't the strong, the rich, the powerful, or the cool people prey upon the weak and the outcast? And why shouldn't the wounded retaliate with guns if they so choose? After all, if we as human beings are nothing more than grown-up goo, what does it matter? Animals will be animals.

It's not my purpose to debate the fallacies of evolution (at least, not in this book). For those who are intellectually honest and want to know the truth about this ideology, the information is widely and easily available. I am simply pointing out that the ultimate issue for the evolutionist is not bones, fossils, and strata—it's *God*. Rejection of God and our accountability to Him is foundational to evolutionist thinking. The rejection of God comes first, and *then* comes the interpretation of the data.

But with God rejected, morality becomes arbitrary. The rights and dignity of others become secondary. Unbridled violence by a Hitler or a Harris, to get what he wants, to guard what is his, or to seek revenge, becomes a perfectly logical alternative.

If a personal, loving Creator God does exist and rule this universe, then we have in Him a transcendent source for meaning, value, sanctity, and dignity, not to mention a fixed and objective point of reference for determining right and wrong—God's Word, the Bible. But if we attempt to remove God from our culture, from our value system, and from our thinking, then we have none of these things, and neither do our children.

My hat is off to authors John H. Hoover and Ronald Oliver, who recognize the relationship between abusive behavior and the absence of spiritual values. In *The Bullying Prevention Handbook,* Hoover and Oliver astutely point out:

> In the end, bullying is related to our ultimate beliefs about the worth of individuals and the way they should be treated. The topics of morality, moral education, ethical reasoning, and spirituality lie at the core of society's problems, including child-on-child aggression. As practitioners think about bullying in the future, it would be beneficial to examine the role that moral development plays in learning to care about one another. Educational leaders may look to the world's religions for answers to the problems of how we interrelate. For

example, the Judeo-Christian-Islamic view that man is created in the image of God has enormous moral implications for how the weakest among us are treated. In the Christian tradition, Jesus stated that whatever was done to the weakest was done to him.[3]

Imagine that! The antidote to our "playground poison" can be found in religious faith and values.

Of course, there are those who would fight this notion tooth and nail, but no matter. We humans can't help proving our need for God most every day, whether we believe in Him or not.

Consider the extremely moving memorial service held in Littleton following the Columbine tragedy. Seventy thousand people attended. The vice president and the governor of Colorado were there, along with other senators, representatives, and dignitaries. Millions more watched on television as Christian artists ministered through music and Franklin Graham delivered a stirring message. Thirteen white doves were released—one for each of the victims. Silver and blue balloons—the Columbine school colors—filled the sky.

With no intention whatsoever of diminishing the solemnity and beauty of that gathering, let me point out something that is going to seem obvious at first: I think it's safe to say that everyone in attendance was in agreement that something horrendously wrong had happened at Columbine High. During the memorial service, people were mourning, crying, lamenting, and sharing a common grief that literally spanned the globe.

But that raises a sticky question: Among the millions of folks who were grieving and agreeing that something wrong had happened, how many, in their normal, everyday lives, believed, talked, taught, and lived by the misguided notion that truth is relative, that there are no moral absolutes, that everyone should decide for him- or herself what is right and wrong? Were there any atheists, evolutionists, or relativists in the crowd?

If the "let's-tear-down-the-rules" crowd is right, and there are no absolutes, no ultimate right and wrong, no transcendent scheme of justice in this universe, then what were those people crying about? According to their world-view, nothing *wrong* happened at Columbine. What happened just *happened*, that's all. Lions eat gazelles, bats eat bugs, and kids shoot kids. What's the big deal?

The truth is, of course, that we all *know* something horrible happened at Columbine. Interesting, isn't it? No matter how adamantly men and women attempt to deny God, we still hint at His existence every time we "get moral" about something.

As Ravi Zacharias explains it (and I'm paraphrasing): In order to say that something is good or evil, you have to have some overall moral scheme, a moral law, by which to figure out what things are good and what things are evil. In order to have a moral law, you have to have a moral law Giver. If there is no moral law Giver, there can be no moral law, and what is, is. You can't make any judgment about it.

And yet we make judgments all the time based on a morality that is, I suggest, beyond ourselves.

Some people may argue that morality is merely a function of culture, that any particular culture develops a morality for the purpose of survival, and that no culture's morality is any better than another's. Then, in almost the same breath, they'll decry Nazi Germany's slaughter of the Jews, the white Europeans' slaughter of the Native Americans, and the burning of widows in some parts of India.

Others might say that our morality has evolved from worse to better: After all, we once had slavery, and now we don't; once women couldn't vote, and now they can; once we trashed the environment, but now we're cleaning it up. But didn't they just say that no particular morality is better than another? By what basis do they fault any agreed-upon morality we may have had in the past? What is, is. What was, was—unless something (or Someone) from somewhere has planted in their hearts a sense of what a better morality would be.

I got a kick out of watching the movie *Contact*, based on the novel by atheist astronomer Carl Sagan. The story deals with the search for intelligent life elsewhere in the universe, and it brings up provocative spiritual and moral issues, sometimes intentionally, and sometimes—I think—by accident. One example is the main character's rationalization for believing that extraterrestrials must be out there someplace: It's such a huge universe that if there's nobody else out there, it would be a terrible waste of space.

If you think about that statement, you quickly realize that it's a moral judgment. It's a good thing to occupy and utilize space; it would be a bad thing to waste all that space. But wait a minute! A moral judgment in an accidental, random, impersonal universe? A waste of space? Who says so? By whose moral standard do we decide what is and isn't a waste of space?

The lead character in *Contact*, played by Jodie Foster, is unfairly bumped from the opportunity to travel to meet the extraterrestrials. It seems her egotistic and ambitious superior has reserved that role for himself. Now we have a moral dilemma because someone has been treated unfairly. But wouldn't it be more consistent with Sagan's atheism to say that the fittest have survived? Funny, isn't it? Avowed atheists and relativists who ardently declare that we should not be encumbered by moral laws still recognize when they have been wronged, and they protest.

We see this same truth wherever two people engage in everyday squabbles and quarrels. Each is convinced of how right he or she is and how wrong the other person is. Imagine a married couple having a fight: Somebody feels he or she has been used, abused, or treated unfairly and the other person had better straighten up. The element of fairness always comes into it.

But who decides what is fair? And where did they ever get the idea that there is such a thing as fairness? Who taught them that?

Even little children know about fairness, and most of them have never taken a philosophy class or majored in theology:

"Johnny, put that cookie away; you'll spoil your supper."

"Well, Susie gets to have one!"

Or . . .

"Sam, it's time for bed."

"But Jimmy gets to stay up!"

Even kids who have not been raised and schooled in

theism still know when they're being ripped off. I suggest that every human being is born with a sense of transcendent justice because every human being, whether they acknowledge it or not, is made in the image of God. God is a moral God, a moral law Giver, and He has written His moral law upon the heart of every human being.

When people try to get around this, it makes for a wacky world. They'll often smack into themselves coming the other way in the same sentence:

"It's wrong to impose your morals on others!"

Uh . . . pardon me, but when you tell me it's wrong to do something, aren't you imposing your morals on me?

"There are no absolutes."

That in itself is an absolute statement.

"No one's moral opinion is valid because we all speak from how we've been indoctrinated."

Well, I guess that would apply to you as well, which means what you've just said isn't valid either.

"Everyone should be able to believe whatever they want!"

Then why are you arguing with me?

"Life is meaningless!"

Would you consider that a meaningful statement?

"You can't know anything for sure."

You seem rather sure about that.

"Students, no view of reality is superior to any other."

Then why are you grading our papers?

"You have no right to say truth is external! We all create our own reality!"

Then I'm *your* fault.

"Oh, here we go again, another right-wing funda-mentalist making bold assertions of fact!"

Pardon me, but didn't you just make a bold assertion of fact?

"There is no right; there is no wrong."

Is that statement right or wrong?

"You can't tell anybody they're wrong."

Am I wrong in doing so?

See what I mean? A lot of this stuff can get pretty silly, especially for those of us who ascribe to a biblical code of ethics. The simple truth is, because objective, external truth and morality exist, we cannot build an argument against objective, external truth and morality without falling back on objective, external truth and morality!

This is why some folks will pontificate about tolerance and open-mindedness and deny absolute truth or morality—until someone crowds in front of them in the grocery checkout line. They will scoff at such antiquated ideas as honor, virtue, and integrity—until their spouse cheats on them or a burglar ransacks their home. Then, suddenly, they will appeal to transcendent absolutes: "That's not fair! I've been cheated, robbed, violated!"

Oh, yeah? Who says?

God says.

God, the external, objective Giver of truth and morality, says that some things are right and some things are wrong. Furthermore, if you examine His Word, you will find that He can be quite specific about what matters to Him. The prophet Micah reminds us, "He has shown you, O man, what is good; and what does the LORD require of you but to do justly, to love mercy, and to walk humbly with your God?" (Mic. 6:8).

God has created us in His image and put each of us here on earth for specific purposes. That means every human being has intrinsic value, preciousness, meaning, and dignity. Why? Because we matter to Almighty God! Moreover, not only is it wrong for me to devalue another person, to belittle, to bully, or to abuse another person created in God's image, I must do what I can to defend those who cannot defend themselves from such abuse. We really are "family," whether or not we choose to admit it.

The Scripture says, "And He has made from one blood every nation of men to dwell on all the face of the earth, and has determined their preappointed times and the boundaries of their dwellings, so that they should seek the Lord, in the hope that they might grope for Him and find Him, though He is not far from each one of us; for in Him we live and move and have our being" (Acts 17:26–28).

God says that it is right to respect my fellowman, to love him, to care for him, and to protect him. It is wrong to abuse, tease, taunt, intimidate, hurt, harass, or violate anyone. Taking it a step further, to demean another person is sin. When we indulge in such practices, we are doing so in direct disobedience to our Lord Jesus Christ. Quoting Old Testament passages found in Deuteronomy and Leviticus, Jesus said, "'You shall love the LORD your God with all your heart, with all your soul, with all your strength, and with all your mind,' and your neighbor as yourself" (Luke 10:27). Don't miss that last part. Another time, Jesus stated it plainly: "Whatever you want men to do to you, do also to them, for this is the Law and the Prophets" (Matt. 7:12).

That's not a bad code to live by.

Help for the Wounded

Chapter Seven

U p to this point in the book I've spoken from my own experience, bringing to light a problem many of us share but have seldom talked about. I've suggested that it's a significant problem that should be talked about and dealt with. I've presented one concise argument— there are plenty of others—that we do have a moral foundation from which we can address the problem.[1]

Just to let you know, this and the following chapters are going to have a common thread you'll see cropping up continually: the whole matter of attitude. If we're going to deal with this problem, it's going to require a change in attitude, not just on the part of the bullies, but also the victims, the schools, society, the powers-that-be, you name it. We've had the wrong attitude about this for too long, and it's time to change it.

Although I'll often be addressing the plight of the young, these chapters aren't just for kids. A wounded spirit has no regard for time or age. Wounded kids grow up to be wounded adults, and wounded adults were most likely wounded kids. Nobody likes being picked on now, nobody liked being picked on as a child, and I've found in my experience and research that *everybody* remembers the hurt and pain associated with being bullied and abused.

When it comes to wounded spirits, three categories of people can relate: those who are wounded, those who wound or have wounded others, and those who fall into both categories—they've been wounded themselves, and they also wound others. This chapter is addressed primarily to the wounded.

When I told a friend of mine that I was writing a book about teasing and peer abuse, he quipped, "Oh, so you're writing a book about *life!*" He had a point there. Quite simply, garbage does happen, and we've all been touched by it in some form at one time or another.

But the questions now are, How do I get over the pain? How do I deal with the wounds inside me? What can I do about the hurtful situation I'm in right now?

Well, let me share some helpful observations and pearls of wisdom with you.

First of all, *if you're wounded, you're not alone.*

Hang on. Before you shrug this little truism off as just another trite phrase or cutesy emotional Band-Aid, please consider how *normal* it makes you.

People come in all shapes and sizes, with all kinds of different abilities *and* disabilities—some are slim, some are fat; others are handsome, ugly, inferior, strong, weak, dorky, or nerdy—but God made us all, so that makes every one of us special, despite our shortcomings. *All* of us have something, or lack something, that potentially can make us a target for abuse.

But that doesn't mean there's something "wrong" with you. Everybody has something they wish they could change about themselves. If you have discovered some "defect" in yourself, welcome to the human race. Regardless of your failures, foibles, or defeats, you're just as human (and just as precious) as anybody else. You're a member.

Think you're ugly? You're a member.

Do you have cystic hygroma, cerebral palsy, muscular dystrophy, or polio? You're a member.

Do you have freckles? Are you too tall, too skinny, too much . . . *anything?* You're a member.

Do you feel left out simply because you're smart? You're a member.

Do you feel left out because you're mentally or physically challenged? You're a member.

Have you ever been raped? Molested? You're still a member.

All of us, with all our wrinkles, shortcomings, bumblings, and imperfections, are God's creation. We're all precious in His sight and should be precious to one another—and don't let anyone tell you otherwise, not even you.

And how about this startling revelation: *It wasn't (isn't) your fault.*

One of the most common mistakes made by victims of abuse is to think that for some reason the abuse was justified, that they actually deserved it. Nothing could be farther from the truth!

This came as a real lightning bolt for me while I was working on this book. As I reluctantly trudged back through my dark, difficult memories and encountered the faces and voices of my abusers once again, I finally saw them for what they were: bullies, not to be feared, but to be pitied. Suddenly it dawned on me: *It wasn't my fault!* What those kids did to me had nothing to do with me. There was never anything so terribly wrong with me that other people had no choice but to be irresistibly, uncontrollably compelled to abuse me. Yes, I was a sinner who needed to be saved by God's grace, but I was not some freak of nature who merited the disdain with which I was treated. It wasn't my problem; it was theirs!

I guess it's just one of those quirky, human tendencies: We tend to believe what others say about us and to view ourselves through their eyes. The moment we get around other people, we start wondering, *Am I okay? Are they going to like me? Will they accept me?* If we manage to make a good impression and everybody seems to like us, we usually go home feeling pretty good about ourselves.

On the other hand, if we stumble or make a blunder, if somebody in the room brands us as the fool or the whole gang of them ignores us entirely, it's quite easy to go home believing we are what they have made us out to be.

When I was in junior high, I was very small for my age. That shouldn't have been a problem, but of course there were those in my class who made it a problem, as if there were something wrong with *me* for being small. Well, I believed it. After all, it was *my* smallness. *I* was the one who brought it to school with me. If I was being heckled, bullied, and thrown around, it was because I deserved it. If I'd just had the common sense to be bigger before coming to school, the other kids would have had no choice but to accept me. No one has the right to be small. I should have known that.

Weird, isn't it? For some reason we focus on ourselves as the cause of the abuse, as if our tormentors have no choice (or responsibility) in the matter, and we buy into their program of lies and humiliation. Before long, we begin thinking, *I'm no good. I'm dumb. I'm a fool. I'm a shrimp. I'm a klutz. That's what the bullies say, so it has to be true!*

Tragically, we can go through the rest of our lives believing those lies. Even as adults, we shy from new relationships, we're afraid of taking risks or being wrong, we get hurt easily, we fumble in conversations, we huddle in a corner at gatherings, and we keep kicking ourselves over every little mistake, because we've been conditioned to believe that *we, of all people, don't have the right to be imperfect.*

Face it. You're not perfect, and that's okay! It's *okay!* Nobody's perfect, and if anybody ever made an issue of it, *they* were the ones in the wrong, not you.

To put it simply, what happened to you shouldn't have happened. What was said about you shouldn't have been said, and what was done to you shouldn't have been done. Nobody deserves to be abused.

So please don't blame yourself.

Now, here's where a change of attitude comes into play, because the third important observation is, *you don't have to put up with it*. You really don't.

And as for whoever is in charge of the school environment, the workplace, the home, or the street, *they shouldn't expect you to*.

Looking back, one of the greatest mysteries of my life is why I did put up with it for so long. I can only explain it this way: I thought I had to. Most of the abuse I endured happened at school. There was no way I could avoid it. After all, it was *school*. While transferring to another school district, attending private school, or homeschooling may be viable options for some families today, these were not options for my family. I was stuck in that one school. My parents made me go. The teachers made me sit at my desk. I was a good kid trying to be obedient. No one ever told me, "Frank, you're in school to learn, not to be picked on and tormented. Teasing and abuse are not part of the package, and we won't allow it. We care about you, so if anyone causes you trouble, let us know."

Here comes that word again: *attitude*. In my case,

parents and teachers simply weren't dealing with abuse—
if they *were*, it sure wasn't on *my* planet. As far as I, the
timid, obedient, little kid, could see or understand, my
parents said I had to be there, the teachers implied
through inaction that it was okay for me to be tormented,
and the unwritten, anti-snitching law among the kids
warned me that I dare not tell anybody. I resigned myself
to enduring the abusive behavior of the bullies in my life
for most of my junior-high and high-school education.

Attitude, attitude, ATTITUDE! We must change our
attitudes regarding this sort of behavior. Those in
authority need to care, and you should expect them to
care. It matters to you, and it should matter to them.
Forget about that foolish, childhood code of silence:
Speak up. Let someone know what's going on, and ask
them—yes, *expect* them—to do something about it. If
you're a kid under someone's legal authority, you still
have rights as a human being. You deserve to be regarded
as God's unique, special creation—because you are!

The same holds true for bullying on the job. If you are
being physically, verbally, or emotionally abused at work,
speak to your supervisor, and if I may suggest it, make it a
matter of productivity and money. If fellow workers are
bullying you, help the supervisor to understand that it's

keeping you from doing your job effectively, and, therefore, it's affecting the smooth operation of the department. Furthermore, it's going to affect the bottom line. The supervisor isn't going to make his numbers because the crew isn't working well as a team, and it's going to be his rear end in the ringer. Any boss, from supervisor to CEO, wants the business to run smoothly and therefore shouldn't stand for such disruptions.

Speak up. You really don't have to tolerate the abuse any longer.

So by now you should be ready to *do something!*

Yes, it's going to take the right attitude on the part of the boss, the teacher, the parent, the principal, or whoever is responsible for the school or work environment. They have to care. They have to be approachable. But you may have to take the first step, at least be ready to respond when you see an opportunity to bring the abuse to the attention of the proper authorities.

For example . . .

It occurred to me the other day that most gym teachers are athletes or former athletes. They were athletes in high school and in college, they naturally hang around other athletes, and now they're at the center of the athletic program at the school. Consequently, some of these men and women haven't a clue what it's like to be a nonathlete, and their physical education program reflects that: The winners get the points, and the losers fall through the cracks; the athletes enjoy the game, and the nonathletes just want to get out of there.

Despite my small stature as a boy, I always enjoyed physical activity and physical challenges. To this day, I exercise, I work out, I enjoy physical labor, and I relish a brisk walk on the logging trails that run through the mountains around our home. I run around and enjoy life outdoors as much as anybody. I'm just not an athlete. I happen to think that tending a garden for all to enjoy, fixing a machine that performs useful labor, and writing books that minister to millions carry more importance for me than putting on little shorts and passing a bouncing, spherical object through a metal hoop more often than the other guy.

For a nonathletic kid, who is already at the bottom of the food chain at most schools, a big, muscular, gruff-voiced, suck-it-up gym teacher with a tight T-shirt and a whistle around his thick neck is the last person on earth he's going to approach about a bullying problem. At the same time, does the gym teacher really know how it feels to be in a world where he has never, and will never, really fit? How are the two going to relate?

I guess that's why I never expected much compassion or mercy from my gym teachers. Most of my P.E. teachers didn't seem to care how I felt; they just yelled at me and blew their whistles. But all that changed when one man, a gym teacher, took the time—a brief moment, actually—to care.

Bullying is a remarkable phenomenon, the way it follows you. In junior high school, I attracted specific people who became my self-appointed tormentors, and that went on for the full three years. When I started high school, I was with a whole new crowd of classmates, and yet the bullying picked up right where it left off. It didn't miss a beat. You'd think the junior-high bullies had held a tie-in meeting with the high-school bullies: "Okay, be looking for Peretti. This is what we've done to him so far . . ."

Remember the young boy in chapter 1? That kind of stuff happened to me all through junior high and all through my sophomore year in high school until suddenly, even astonishingly, everything changed. I don't remember the exact times and dates, but I do remember the chain of events. It started one day when I was running an errand for my mom.

The Graham Street Grocery was a little neighborhood grocery store less than a block from our house. We had an account there, and Mom often sent me to pick up small items: a loaf of bread, milk, ice cream, whatever. A young man from my high school got an after-school job there, and though I'd never done him wrong and he hardly knew me, he became my enemy. I guess, to him, it was the cool thing to do.

On this particular day, I was minding my own business, just going up and down those short little aisles and picking up items on my grocery list, when my nemesis met me toward the back of the store, out of his boss's earshot.

"Whatcha doin', Peretti?"

"Oh, just buying some stuff."

"What do you need?"

I looked at my list. "I need to get some deodorant."

"Which kind?"

You know deodorants. There are so many different brands, they can fill a whole shelf. "Well, we usually use this one. . . ."

He grabbed a can off the shelf. "This one?"

I thought he was going to hand it to me. "Yeah."

Suddenly, without provocation, he popped the cap off and sprayed the deodorant directly in my face! I forget what he said as he did it, but it wasn't kind.

That stuff stings! My eyes were watering, and tears streamed down my face. I was shocked and incredulous.

I just couldn't believe a guy waiting on me in a grocery store would do that to me! I quickly made my way to the checkout counter, rubbing my eyes and wiping my nose. I could hardly see as I signed our tab and made a hasty exit from the store.

You may well ask why I didn't report the incident to Vern, the man who owned the store. Looking back, I can only wonder the same. It must have had something to do with the devious power of that old maxim that has protected bullies for generations: You don't snitch.

I stumbled out of the store and around the corner, my grocery bag in my arm, and then . . . it's hard to describe . . . I was like a hunted animal who has been shot but still runs several yards before collapsing from loss of blood. I made it around the corner, but that's as far as I could go before something just broke inside me. I dropped to the curb, weeping, devastated, despondent. I'd come to the end.

"Oh, dear Lord," I prayed, still wiping the sting out of my eyes. "Please . . . I just can't take it anymore." It felt just a little strange to be praying such a thing because, in my mind, I still linked God with all the other authorities in my life. They were all making me go through this, and so was He. As I prayed, I was actually pleading for mercy. "Please, God; please don't do this to me anymore. Don't make me go back there. Have mercy, dear Lord. I haven't fought back; I haven't snitched; I've turned the other cheek. Haven't I suffered enough?"

I'm reminded of God's response to Moses: "Surely I have heard the cry of My people in Egypt." They'd been crying to Him for the better part of four hundred years! But, at last, it was God's time to answer.

And, after so, so, long, God answered me.

A few days later, I faithfully and obediently stepped through the big, ominous door for another hour of Boy's Hell. My despair must have been showing. One of the teachers paused—he actually took just a moment—and spoke quietly to me. "How you doing? You feeling okay?"

I looked back at him in disbelief. Somebody in authority was actually asking about me, and he seemed genuinely concerned! He wasn't even *my* teacher. He had other classes, other coaching duties, but he was there, and he had noticed that I was looking ill. This was so unexpected, so unusual, I didn't know what to say, or whether I should say anything at all. I was afraid of those gruff P.E. teachers. Not one of them had ever, *ever* before asked me how I felt.

I muttered some look-down-at-the-floor answer, just as

an insecure boy my age might do, and he went on about his business.

But the gentle tone of his voice did something to me: It gave me just the tiniest, years-in-coming ray of hope, something I'd never felt before. Somebody really wanted to know how I was doing? Somebody might really listen? I grabbed onto that hope for all I was worth, and then, suddenly, an idea came to me. I didn't think I could express myself orally to a teacher who still intimidated me, but by now, I knew I could write. I decided to write my gym teacher a letter. I would tell him everything. Maybe things *could* change.

The first chance I got—study hall, I think it was—I started drafting a letter. I can vividly remember sitting in the quiet of the library on the third floor of Cleveland High School in Seattle, addressing a letter to Mr. Sampson, my P.E. teacher. First of all, I let him know that it was the kind inquiry of his colleague that prompted my letter, and then I began. I wrote that whole period. I wrote during lunch. I wrote during any opportunity I could find the rest of the day. I chronicled everything I could remember: all the insults, the abuse, the assaults, the humiliations, everything over the past several years. The letter filled several pages, handwritten in blue ink, single-spaced, both sides of the paper. That afternoon, before leaving for home, I went into the school office and slipped it into Mr. Sampson's mailbox.

Gym class was every other day, so he had a day to read my letter before I had to face him again. By the time I came through that door the next time, Mr. Sampson was looking for me. "Peretti. Hold up a second," he called from inside his locker-room office.

Well, Mr. Sampson had obviously read my letter. Now what? He didn't seem very angry. Who else had seen that letter? What if he wanted to read the letter in front of the other guys in the locker room? *Oh, Lord, this is it. Please don't let me down.*

I stood there against the wall, nervous, schoolbooks in my hand, a stream of boys passing before me on their way to the locker room. From my vantage point, I could see through the office door. Mr. Sampson was talking on the phone, and I just barely made out the words, "You want to see him now?"

See who? Me? Who wanted to see me?

He hung up the phone, filled out a hall pass, and sent me to the school office to see the counselor, Mr. Eisenbrey. I'd always been afraid of Mr. Sampson, and I'd always been afraid of Mr. Eisenbrey, but that day changed everything. Those guys had compassion on me; they really did care.

Mr. Eisenbrey had reviewed my letter and was actually warm and cheerful as he helped me rework my class schedule, excusing me from P.E. for the remainder of the school year. "We'll just call it a medical excuse," he said, scribbling some notes on a piece of paper. He signed me off and sent me back to Mr. Sampson so he could sign the forms too.

Mr. Sampson didn't say anything as he filled out the form on his ever-present clipboard. He just smiled at me.

When he handed me my class transfer, my *parole*, I told him, "If you were a girl, I'd kiss you!"

"You're welcome," was all he said.

I went out that door and never saw the inside of that locker room again.

I can't overstate the pivotal nature of that day in my life. From that moment onward, everything was so different. I could enjoy school. I could get excited about being a Cleveland Eagle. I bought a red-and-white pennant and put it on my bedroom wall. I donned my red-and-white Cleveland beanie, went to the football games, and felt great about my school. I got involved in school drama productions—where I could actually use some of the gifts

God had given me—and I *burst* out of my shell, making lots of new friends, and just going nuts being creative. For the first time in my life, I began to enjoy being *me!*

So, I said all that to say this: I hope someone in your school, or workplace, or *wherever*—maybe someone you don't even suspect would be kind—will be kind to you. I hope they will have the caring, compassionate attitude that is necessary to bring about a change. I hope you will speak to that person, or do as I did and write a letter. Talk about it. I understand that the custom, the expectation, the legacy of our culture up to this point has been to keep it to yourself. Listen, if you think you need some kind of permission to bring up the subject and deal with it, *I give you that permission.* You needn't hide behind the facade of having it all together any longer. Get help! Talk to someone who cares—and don't go another day carrying the burden alone.

If possible, *become a one-to-one peacemaker.*

Granted, some bullies are not the reasonable type. They pick on you because they are warped and maladjusted. For any number of reasons—a dysfunctional family, low self-esteem, low achievement, too much lead in their drinking water, or some other malady, real or imagined—they think they have to push their weight around in order to feel better about themselves. Unless they have a major turnaround in their lives, they'll either wind up in prison or become DMV license examiners.

But for the most part, bullies are human beings just like you and me, and sometimes they can be reached with a little bit of honesty and friendship—if you can talk with them one-on-one. I've known a few bullies who were actually very intelligent A students, who went on to be successful adults. Oftentimes, the reason they allowed themselves to become cruel and insensitive was because of the crowd; it was the "cool" thing to do.

Consider going to that person and having a private discussion with him, away from his friends. Be sincere, kind, and honest, and lay the issues on the table: You would rather be friends than enemies, and what he is doing is hurtful to you. If you have done something to offend him, apologize and make it right. If you've done nothing to offend him, ask him why he wants to hurt you.

Attempt to get to know the person who has been bullying you. In nine cases out of ten, the bully doesn't even know the person he's picking on. If he really knew the victim as a person instead of as a punching bag, he might ease up. And who knows? You could end up being friends.

Perhaps you and the bully have a mutual friend or acquaintance to whom you could appeal for help. I remember sitting at lunch with a friend named Paul in junior high school, and I started sharing my problems with him.

"*Who's* picking on you?" he asked.

I didn't have any trouble thinking of a name. I could even point the guy out, sitting across the lunchroom. "He's really mean. He just won't leave me alone."

Paul was astonished. "*Neil?* Are you sure?"

I told Paul what Neil had been doing to me in the locker room during gym class, and Paul shook his head, perplexed. He was genuinely surprised and dismayed to hear about the way Neil had been treating me. "But Neil's a nice guy."

"Well, he sure isn't nice to me."

The next time I encountered Neil in the locker room, he was friendly. He complimented the sweater I was wearing. He never badgered, bullied, or bothered me again.

It's easy to figure out what happened behind the scenes. Paul went to Neil and told him, "Hey, Frank's a decent guy. He's a friend of mine. You don't want to pick on him."

Attitude. Sometimes a bully is a "nice guy," too, who

just needs to be awakened to the fact that his victim is a person, maybe even a likable person. Once confronted, if he has the moral fiber and some common decency, he'll change his behavior.

Certainly, one of the most important steps toward healing of a wounded spirit is to *forgive*. It can be tough to do, but if you don't forgive those individuals who have hurt you in the past, bitterness will eat you alive and rob you of a peaceful future. You'll be granting the bullies the power to take away your happiness and to make you feel rotten when *they aren't even there!* Let it go. God will give you the grace you need, if you will make the conscious choice to forgive. Throw off those chains of bitterness and resentment that have been constraining you for so long, and get on with your life.

Finally, take heart: *A wounded spirit need not be permanent.* Please understand: It's never too late to start doing the right thing; it's never too late to change for the better. Especially if you're young, life as you know it right now is not fixed in cement. As we grow, we change, our circumstances change, and we find ourselves in different places and situations. Through it all, God has a purpose and a plan for your life. He made you the way you are for a reason, and don't worry, you are going to find out what it is. You're going to be okay.

When I was a kid, I felt terrible about myself. My self-image was in the toilet because I couldn't throw or catch a football, I couldn't run very fast, and I was considered small and frail for my age. Today, I'm an adult; I'm an author and a public speaker, I play in a talented acoustic band, I fly my own plane, I have a lovely wife, and a comfortable home tucked in the woods on the side of a mountain, and frankly, I don't cry too much about the fact that I still can't throw or catch a football.

Every once in a while, as I sit back in our living room, looking out the large picture windows and admiring the majestic grandeur and beauty of the snowcapped mountains, I wonder how many of those big, brutal jocks I once knew are now limping from old sports injuries. I can't help but smile as I picture some of those big lugs reporting to a smaller-framed boss who has a better-developed brain and a much bigger office! As Bill Gates has said, "Don't pick on the nerds. You'll probably end up working for one."

God does have a way of evening things out.

Just follow His way. Live your life well, according to His principles. He'll take care of the rest.

For Those
Who Wound

Chapter Eight

Okay, it's time to confess; I need to come clean on some things. Up until now, I've been writing mostly from the perspective of the victim, which puts me in a safe place. I can be the sweet, innocent hero of the story, while all the other characters are the bad guys. Well, it was nice while it lasted, but in real life there is always another side to the story. Whether we regard ourselves as bully or victim, the Bible is quite correct when it tells us that "all have sinned and fall short of the glory of God" (Rom. 3:23). Truth be told, bully or victim, we're all made of the same stuff. We're all capable of the same things.

Have I ever wounded anyone? Yes, I'm sorry to say that I have. I never considered myself the bullying type—with the small-framed body I had, badgering or pushing other people around physically wasn't much of an option for me—but there were times when I could say mean things. I could spread malicious gossip, cut people down with insults, or go along with the crowd by ostracizing someone. It's so easy to do, and it amazes me how a victim, who knows how it feels, can still be insensitive to the feelings of others. Know what I'm talking about?

So . . . ouch! This could get uncomfortable, but let's be honest with ourselves and allow God to change us as we work through this chapter together. Most of us have been wounded by other people, some of us have *wounded* others, and some of us have not only been wounded, but for whatever reason, don't get a clue, and go on to wound others!

As with most other aspects of sin, wounding other people comes naturally. We don't feel the pain as we dish it out, so—here it comes again—we go along with the attitude that says, "It's no big deal. All my friends are picking on so-and-so, and I want to be accepted as one of the group. I want them to like me, and I want to be like them. Everybody does it. It's the thing to do."

We know better, yet somehow this type of abusive behavior falls outside our definition of *sin*.

So let's rethink that definition. Based on what the Bible, or even your God-given conscience, tells you, wouldn't you say it's wrong to hurt, injure, or abuse another human being? Is it wrong to mock, tease, or bully people, hurting them, violating their personhood, and destroying their dignity?

Need I say more?

But even Christians wound.

For example, let's talk about all those squeaky clean, born-again students attending Christian colleges. Hey, they know their Bibles. They worship and pray at all the chapel services. They're out to spread the good news of Jesus Christ and change their world for the glory of God.

And yet, when you get a chance to observe the social fabric on campus, it's sad to discover things haven't changed much since junior and senior high school. The upperclassmen—yes, those fine men and women who claim to be followers of Christ—find it easy to put the underclassmen in their place. The jocks laugh and needle the nonathletes; the girls establish their social cliques and close the door to outsiders. Derogatory names and rumors float around freely. The very mention of certain names produces snickers among the elite in the student lounge.

On any college campus, it's normal to find a particular type of young male who takes great pride in his physical prowess and virility but seems stunted when it comes to character. He shoots baskets to show the world he can toss a ball through a hoop but doesn't help the kid who would like to learn; he presses iron to show the world how much weight he can lift but never thinks of coaching anyone else; he flexes his muscles to show the world he has bulging biceps and disrespects anyone who doesn't.

I encountered a young man of this description some time ago, and he was the quintessential bullying jock. I'd never before seen someone purposely wearing a tight muscle shirt and flexing his muscles at everybody. I thought only professional wrestlers on television did that! This guy could even make his neck bigger than his head, and he was really proud of that.

Unfortunately, along with all those muscles came an

attitude. This fellow had the idea that his finely chiseled, powerful physique entitled him to be the king in any group, and he was more than willing to use his brawn to get that point across. I saw him grab a smaller guy, lift him off his feet, and pin him against the wall, purely to intimidate him. Now mind you, these were not children in junior high or youths in high school; this incident took place among young men at a Christian college! I must have been naive at the time, because it shocked me so severely that I didn't say a word.

In retrospect, I think about the film A *Few Good Men*, featuring Tom Cruise, Demi Moore, and Kevin Pollak. Jack Nicholson plays Colonel Jessup, the bad guy. Don't take your kids to see it—the language gets a little salty— but that movie has powerful moral lessons that apply here. The story involves two marines, stationed at the Guantanamo military base in Cuba, who are ordered by their superior officer to carry out a "code red" on a fellow marine. A "code red" is an unofficial, even illegal form of discipline that can take the form of a beating, hazing, head shaving, or any other humiliation, and the purpose is to "encourage" a foul-up to get his act together. The foul-up in this case is a weakling named

Willie who, for undetected but legitimate medical reasons, is having trouble running, breathing, and keeping up with the other soldiers in the stifling Cuban heat. Unfortunately, as Willie's "encouragers" try to beat him into shape, Willie's medical condition brings about his death, and the two marines are put on trial for murder.

Thus arise some great moral issues and some great quotes.

The defendants' lawyers, played by Tom Cruise, Demi Moore, and Kevin Pollak, work together as a team even though they are divided regarding the marines' innocence. Tom Cruise thinks the two marines are innocent because they were following orders, but Kevin Pollak feels that is no excuse: "I believe every word of their story—and I think they ought to go to jail for the rest of their lives."

It is no secret that Pollak's character has no sympathy for two tough marines who, even though following orders, killed a fellow marine. When Moore's character asks him, "Why do you hate them so much?" Pollak responds, "They beat up on a weakling! That's all they did, all right? The rest of this is just smoke-filled, coffeehouse crap! They tortured and tormented a weaker kid! They didn't like him, so they killed him, and why? 'Cause he couldn't run very fast!"

The issue leaps out from the movie screen: the strong preying upon the weak.

But then, within seconds, the other side of the issue, the *answer* to the issue, also leaps from the screen when Pollak asks Moore, "Why do you *like* them so much?" and she responds, "Because they stand on the wall, and they say, 'Nothing's going to hurt you tonight, not on my watch.'"

The strong *protecting* the weak. Yes!

As the trial ends, the marines are acquitted of murder, but they are convicted of conduct unbecoming a marine and are sentenced to be dishonorably discharged from the Marine Corps. The younger marine protests, "I don't understand. Colonel Jessup said he ordered the code red. What did we do wrong? We did nothing wrong!"

But the older, wiser marine responds, "Yeah, we did. We were supposed to fight for people who couldn't fight for themselves. We were supposed to fight for Willie."

By this point in the movie, I get tearful. Yes. This is the answer. This is what it's all about. The filmmakers have addressed something that we who spend most of our lives in safe Christian confines rarely confront: Namely, the depth of a person's character is not measured by his or her physical strength, but by the depth of his or her nobility. How do we treat those who are weaker?

Have you ever replayed an incident in your mind the way you'd like it to have happened? Here's my replay of that scene with Mr. Muscles and his victim on the Christian college campus:

I'd step up to that big lug, look him right in the eyes (when you're a white-bearded wise guy pushing fifty years of age, you can do stuff like that), and I'd ask him, "Just what in the world do you think you're doing? You unhand him immediately!"

And then I'd grab a telephone—in my mental replay, a phone is always handy—and tell that musclehead, "See this phone in my hand? Young man, you have a choice. Either you sit down and listen to a lecture, or I dial the police and file a criminal complaint against you for assault. Which will it be?"

He agrees to the lecture, so there *are* some brains buried under there somewhere. Having his undivided attention, I tell him, "It's time you seriously considered why God gave you all that strength and physical superiority. It wasn't so you could abuse, oppress, and violate those who aren't as strong as you are. He gave you that strength so you could *defend and protect* those who are weaker, fight for those who can't fight for themselves, and stand between the defenseless and anyone or anything that might harm them. Remember the biblical cities with the wall around them, and how guardians would stand on that wall to protect the people inside the city? That's what God has called you to do.

"Any gift you receive from God is not for yourself, but for others. The strong are strong to protect the weak; those with abundance are blessed so they can help the needy; the smart and the wise are gifted to help the befuddled and foolish.

"The measure of a man is not his strength; it is the depth of his nobility. The measure of any person is how he or she treats those who are less gifted, less intelligent, and less able. The measure of a Christian is how willing he or she is to reach down and help those who are less fortunate—to take the strength and advantage they have to help those who have not.

"God has gifted you with strength. You should thank Him for that privilege by standing on that wall and telling others, 'Don't worry. Nobody's gonna hurt you, not on my watch.'"

In my best replays, the now former bully and his

victim become best friends and both go out to change the world for Christ . . . hey, it could happen!

On a recent book tour, I stopped in at a major Chicago newspaper to be interviewed by their religion editor, a pleasant gentleman with whom I immediately felt comfortable. We discussed my book *The Visitation* for a while, going through the obligatory questions and answers, and then, perhaps because he walked with the aid of crutches, we got on the subject of abuse, teasing, and harassment. He shared with me how, when he was growing up, the other kids gave him no end of teasing and harassment because of his polio.

"You still feel it, don't you?" I asked him.

He nodded. "Oh, yes." He was in his sixties.

I was even more impressed with the reporter when he told me about his two sons. Both of them are big, strong fellows, and throughout their childhood, he taught them to put their strength to use in standing up for the weak and defending those who cannot defend themselves. Because of their father's experience with polio, they grew up with a unique sensitivity regarding their own gifts and the needs of others. The reporter raised his sons to be protectors, rather than bullies. Now that's the way things ought to be.

I told you that I never forgot the names and the faces of those who hurt me. There's one other name and one other face I will remember all my life, but for the opposite reason. I won't give you his full name, but his first name was John. It was a classic situation, commonplace and sadly predictable: I was a pitiful creature in my gym class, and some character with a truckload of dysfunction in his life came after me. Well, John happened to be there, and he stepped in. He had a size advantage, he was strong, and he was quite persuasive. With an assertive presence and a calm voice, he convinced Mr. Dysfunction that there were better things to do and better places to be, and Mr. D bought his argument. I don't recall that Mr. D ever bothered me again.

More than thirty years later, I still remember John, and I pray for him whenever I think of that moment. He came between me and harm. He stood on that wall. I think he's the only one who ever did.

We need more people like John in this world, and you may be that kind of person, or at least somebody who can become one. Perhaps, up to this point, you've been a teaser, a source of pain rather than a source of comfort. You can change all that. All it takes is a decision, a pivotal moment when you decide you will put a stop to the bullying and abuse and begin treating everyone who passes your way as a priceless, precious, miraculous creation of God, a person for whom Jesus Christ bled and died, a person who matters to God just as much as you do.

The first step is to wake up to what you've done and what you may still be doing. Admit your sins honestly before God, ask Him for forgiveness, and then declare that from this day forward, with God's help, your bullying and malicious teasing days are over. You will begin to treat every person as valuable, even sacred.

Grownup, do you remember being a teaser and abuser when you were in school? As you entered adult life, did you ever stop? Have you ever apologized to those people you hurt? Have you ever let go of those childish ways, or have you merely found new faces and bodies to demean? Now is the time to break with the past and start afresh. Right now, right where you are, can you remember the people you've tormented?

I can tell you with great certainty that *they* remember *you*. It's a sobering thought. I know how abuse in my youth hurt me deeply and still affects me today, and I've met several folks who can relate to my experience because they've suffered similarly.

But now flip it around: How many folks out there in the world, most of them my age, are still living with the effects of the teasing *I* dished out at *them*? How many people are still wounded because of what you or I did to them?

I can see the faces of some of the people I hurt. How about you? How many faces can *you* count?

Young person, are you inflicting wounds on others? What kind of memories do you want to live with? Will you really be proud of yourself for teasing that person who is weaker than you are in some way? Is your self-esteem so low that you must step on somebody else to feel good about yourself? How do you want people to remember you—as a lowlife bully who wallowed in self-delusion, or as a courageous friend who stood nobly on the wall, who stood up for what was right, and who defended those who could not defend themselves? These tough questions need honest answers.

Second, you need to go to God for cleansing. If we confess our sins—sure, you know the rest—He'll forgive us and cleanse us from all unrighteousness (see 1 John 1:9). But we need to take it a step further. Here's what I've done: I've gone to the Lord in prayer and asked Him to bring to my mind the folks I've hurt. Then I've apologized to the Lord, in prayer, and I've apologized to them, asking God to grant each person the grace to forgive me and to help them find healing in their lives.

Third, just as I have done, ask God to change your heart and make you like Jesus. Consider how Scripture describes Him in Matthew 12:20: "A battered reed He will not break off, and a smoldering wick He will not put out" (NASB). Jesus never took cruel advantage of anyone's disadvantage. The bruised, He helped. The weak and dying, He renewed. That's what I want to do; that's how I want to be.

Fourth, you might consider a new way of thanking God for whatever advantages He has given you: your physical strength, your intelligence, your sense of humor, your reputation, that position on the cheerleading squad or the football team, or the opened doors of opportunity at your job.

You can thank Him by putting your gift into service on behalf of others. You can become, in your own way, the guardian who stands on the wall and says to those who are weaker, smaller, and less advantaged, "Don't you worry. Nobody's going to hurt you, not on my watch."

To borrow from Shakespeare, it's time to "grace this latter age with noble deeds." Rather than flaunting our gifts, our success, our popularity, our privilege, we should realize that it's time to be noble and consider those gifts for what they are: our means, our resources by which we are to help others.

Now it's my turn.

Wounding can be so easy, and the line between playful teasing and thoughtless tormenting can become dangerously blurred. I could try to rationalize that my teasing was the playful variety, but as I look back on it, I have to admit that some of the kids I teased were not laughing along.

It's so easy not to think about what you're doing as you join with others in selecting that one person who doesn't quite fit. It's so easy to join in the mockery and the gossip rather than come to that person's defense.

I can still see the faces and remember the names of those who tormented me. But I can also remember some of the names and faces of young men and women toward whom I was less than a friend. I have to wonder how they feel about what I and others said about them and how that may have affected the course of their lives.

May I go on record?

Friend, if you remember Frank Peretti teasing you or hurting you in any way, I want to say I'm sorry. Sure, I've thought about it at other times, but the writing of this book has brought me face to face with my own culpability, and I repent and apologize. There were words that came from my mouth that I wish I could recapture and banish forever. There were moments when I wasn't there for you and should have been. There were times I sided against you, when I knew that side was in the wrong.

Friend, you didn't deserve it. Please forgive me, and may God grant you grace to forgive any others who have hurt you as I did. May you find freedom from pain and bitterness and healing as we grow together in God's unconditional love.

Things Could Be Different

Chapter Nine

A separate room had been prepared for the boys. It was cold and impersonal, like a prison; the echoing, concrete walls had been painted dirty beige, then marred and chipped over the years, then painted again. The walls were bare except for posted rules, warnings, and advisories, and the only windows were high against the ceiling, caged behind iron grillwork thickly wrapped in paint, rust, and more paint. The air was dank, tainted with the odors of steam, sweat, and skin. Years of rust and sediment from the dripping showerheads and armies of bare, wet feet had marbled the floor with streaks and patches of reddish brown.

The boy was nervous and afraid on his first day through that big door. He was small, nonathletic, and timid. He'd never been in this place, or anywhere like this place, before. Though he excelled in academics and felt comfortable in most any classroom, to him this was a different, threatening world, a world of muscles, workouts, sports, and sweat. As he lined up along the lockers with the other boys his age, he could see some of them sizing him up. "Hi, wimp," one of them said, a sneer curling his lip.

"Hey!" It was the teacher's assistant, a few grades older, overseeing the lineup. He went over to the kid who'd spoken and got right in his face. "You don't do that in here."

The name-caller was about to come back with something, but a shrill whistle made him jump.

It was the gym teacher, Mr. Akers, entering the locker room like an officer coming on deck. "All right, silence! Everybody, eyes forward, straight and at attention!"

He got immediate compliance, and with good enough reason. This guy was built like a tank, and his expression made it clear he was not to be trifled with. He carried a clipboard. He had a whistle around his neck. He wore a tight T-shirt. He carried a baseball bat planed flat, the perfect implement for administering swats.

"Mr. Lane will take the roll."

The teacher's assistant, Bruce Lane, called out the names of the students and checked them off as they answered, "Here." All through the roll call, Mr. Akers stood there with his clipboard and his swatter, studying every face.

When the roll call ended, he said, "At ease. Have a seat on the benches, fellows. Make room over there. Let's go."

They sat down facing him. He leaned against the wall, one foot flat on the wall behind him so that his knee extended, forming a desk for his clipboard. "Gentlemen, welcome to my class. On your class schedule you see this hour designated as '*Physical* Education,' but let me assure you, this class will involve more than just your bodies. Any education worthy of the name doesn't just build the body or the mind; it also builds character. So you'll need more than a strong body and athletic skill to excel in this class—sorry to disappoint some of you. You'll need to apply your minds and your spirits as well.

"It is our hope that you'll leave here healthier and more physically fit than when you first came in. But it is also our hope that you'll leave here having improved the personal qualities you'll need in every other area of your lives: discipline, perseverance, the ability and willingness to work as a team, and a sportsmanlike attitude.

"If you enjoy competition, I encourage you to turn out for the basketball, baseball, football, tennis, or soccer teams. I assure you, in those programs you will have every opportunity to one-up the guy on the opposing team and show everybody what a great athlete you are. In this class, the only person you'll be competing against is yourself. We're going to help you set reasonable goals for improving your fitness, strength, and stamina, and then we're going to do all we can to help you achieve those goals.

"Now as you look around the room, you'll notice that human beings come in all sizes and shapes, all different levels of strength and ability. I want to emphasize that none of that matters here. Regardless of your size or physical maturity, each and every one of you deserves the chance to feel proud of what you can accomplish. That's why we're going to be a team. We're going to think as a team, act as a team, and learn as a team. We expect you to help each other out, to cheer for each other, to do all you can to help your teammates rise to the top of their potential."

Mr. Akers toyed with the ominous, flattened baseball bat as he looked every boy in the eye. "That's why we do not tolerate bullies in this class. We do not allow teasing, harassment, put-downs, one-upmanship, or the mistreatment of any teammate by another." He paused to let that sink in, and then added, "You will maintain sportsmanlike conduct at all times, showing courtesy and respect for your teammates."

The boy had come into this class feeling timid and afraid, but by the time Mr. Akers had finished his orientation remarks, he could see he had an advocate if he ever needed one. He was starting to feel safe.

In the weeks that followed, Mr. Akers and his assistants worked with each class member, planning out a physical fitness program appropriate to each boy's capability. Because of his small stature and clumsiness, the boy had always been intimidated by any sport that threw him among bodies bigger than he was. The workout room with its treadmill, stair stepper, and weight machine appealed to him, because he could work on his own, without embarrassment.

"Just remember," Mr. Akers told him, "you're not here to be like somebody else. You're here to improve yourself and to help the others do the same."

With encouragement from Mr. Akers, the young man set reasonable goals for himself. With encouragement from his classmates, he exceeded those goals. On the last day of the semester, he cheered for his classmates, and they cheered for him.

He didn't think he'd ever look forward to gym class, but by semester's end, he decided he could enjoy P.E. class. He even liked Mr. Akers.

Well, we all like happy endings, but is this one realistic? I believe it can be. All it takes is a change in attitude on the part of parents, principals, teachers, and others in positions of authority. We teach our children to say please and thank you, not to burp at the table, to share, to clean up their rooms; we try to educate them to stay off drugs and to abstain from sex outside of marriage. Why do we not teach them, from the very beginning, the sanctity of human life, the dignity of the individual, the responsibility we have to respect and safeguard our fellowman? Why aren't such ideals made perfectly clear to the students in the halls of our schools?

From the outset, on the very first day of school, the

principal should address the entire student body and let them know that teasing, harassment, bullying, and abuse absolutely will not be tolerated—and yes, that would include upperclassmen picking on underclassmen. A senior razzing a freshman may seem cute and traditional, but all it really does is divide two human beings who could have been friends and helped each other. It also sets a "tradition" that opens wide the doors of cruelty, that tells the students it's fun and okay to make someone's life miserable.

Whatever attitude the school leadership displays will trickle down through the student body. If teasing a younger kid is okay, then having no regard for the feelings of others is okay. If the principal and teachers remain aloof and indifferent toward bullying, the kids will remain indifferent and simply watch as it goes on all around them. If the gym teacher is cruel, brutal, and unapproachable, the boys in his gym class will be the same way toward each other, equating brutality with manliness and depriving our world of that many more *true* men.

Imagine a school that openly, directly enforces a zero-tolerance, anti-bullying policy, instructing and encouraging kids to call witnesses and to back each other up when a bullying incident occurs. Imagine students being instructed that they are responsible for their fellow human beings and that it is right and noble to get involved when someone is being hurt. Imagine a student being able to attend school knowing that his or her classmates, whether friend or stranger, are there for them if the need should ever arise.

If the school leadership, from the outset, establishes a policy of mutual respect at all levels and backs it up with rules, instruction, procedures, and *example*, we just might have a safer, more ennobling school environment and a few more compassionate human beings walking our streets after graduation.

Who knows? Such a refreshing attitude might just spill over into our families, into the workplace, our churches, and civic groups, making it a better "playground" for all of us.

Please take this matter of bullying seriously. You were a kid once. Would you want your child to suffer the taunts you had to suffer? Have you really forgotten how it felt?

Imagine this situation: A loving husband approaches his wife from behind her back, puts his arms around her, and calls her a particular nickname just to be funny.

Suddenly, she turns on him, lashes him up one side and down the other, and breaks into tears. When the smoke and shrapnel finally settle and he has prepared an ice pack to put over his black eye, she informs him that she was always called that name in grade school and she hated it, hated it, hated it!

Well, okay, he won't call her that name again, but even so, the incident has smacked them both in the head with one realization: That stuff comes back. When we've been hurt, tormented, abused, or teased as children, we still have raw spots that remain into our adulthood. We remember how it feels, and we don't like it when people in the grown-up world—a friend, a spouse, a traffic cop, a crabby clerk—treat us the way we were treated years ago. Ever have a friend, spouse, or associate throw a little stinger your way? Perhaps they called you a name similar to the one you hated in grade school. Perhaps they called attention to a physical characteristic for which you paid dearly when you were young. Maybe they made a snide comment about the clothes you were wearing or the way you combed your hair. Part of you feels as if you're right back on that grade school playground or in that junior-high hallway all over again. That wounded child is still inside you.

So think twice, parents, before you shrug off your child's suffering as something he or she will just have to go through and outgrow. Did you ever, *really* outgrow it?

A close friend of mine who never cared to go to men's retreats finally gave in and attended one not too long ago. He came back deeply affected by what he saw and heard.

All the men, about a hundred in number, were given an assignment for the weekend: to write a poem about something that affected them deeply and emotionally. Through this exercise, each man was able to share his vulnerable side with sympathetic peers. The poems spoke of precious things as well as painful: the birth of the first child and the death of a child, the finding of true love and the loss of a spouse, a special praise from a parent and a crushing disappointment in a parent.

With a hundred men contributing, the group saw a kaleidoscope of life, and they realized how life can, at times, be so kind and so cruel.

During the last evening of the weekend retreat, a successful businessman in his forties stood to address the group. As he began to read his poem, he broke down weeping. He'd never talked to anyone about it before, but for him, one of the most painful experiences of his life was being overweight as a kid and being mocked and ridiculed about it in school. The teasing was merciless and it never let up, year after year. It framed his entire concept of himself, a concept he carried well into adulthood, and it was only now, when he felt safe among the other guys, that he could face it.

He sat down, and a brief, awkward silence enveloped the room, as if the men were wondering, *What can we do for this guy? What can we say? After all, it all happened so long ago.*

The next man stepped to the front to share his poem, but he was weeping before he could even unfold the poem to read it. He looked at the forty-year-old businessman and confessed, "Brother, when I was a kid, I was one of those who picked on kids like you. I thought it was fun. I guess it made me feel cool, like I was somebody. But I want to tell you, it was wrong, and until right now I've never faced up to it. Brother, I need to ask your forgiveness. I'm sorry. Please forgive me."

He embraced the businessman, and the room fell silent once again. Some other men started crying. In a coincidence so remarkable that it had to be a "divine appointment," two kids from different backgrounds and different schoolyards, the wounder and the wounded, had found each other and were making things right. The room was shaken.

See? We remember.

So parents and teachers, please talk about it. Bring up the subject yourself if your kids don't. Let your children know that they don't have to put up with bullying and abusive treatment and that there are steps they can take to prevent it. My parents didn't know the full extent of what I was suffering because I never said anything. I never said anything because it would be snitching, and, for all I knew, nothing could be done about it anyway. I never heard any teacher, counselor, or principal at my schools say that teasing and abuse were wrong. Not one teacher ever stepped in to prevent it. I even heard one teacher ask a friend of mine, "What's the matter—those guys picking on you?" The teacher then laughed about it, walked away, and did nothing. But he sent his message: "You're on your own, bub. You won't get any help from me."

In the aftermath of Littleton, we heard so much talk and fretting about "looking for the signs" that might lead kids to resort to violence. How can we know? What should we look for?

To this I say, *Wake up to wounded spirits!* A bruise or a

cut is visible, but a wounded spirit can remain buried deep inside a person unless you provide the environment that will bring it out and heal it. The letter I wrote to Mr. Sampson was my final act of desperation. Thankfully, the pen was mightier than the gun, but I've often wondered what might have happened, had not that one special teacher paused to ask me how I was doing. Believe me, there are kids in your school, and maybe right in your home, who have a story to tell.

And yes, you as an adult may also have a story to tell, and it may not be a tale about the bullies of your youth. It may involve the bullies you have to put up with in the adult world. As research has found, bullies in school often go on to be bullies at home and at work (see the resource list in the back of this book for research supporting this fact). Have you ever had a boss—even a *Christian* boss—who doesn't mind belittling his or her employees in front of coworkers, spouting obscenities at them, and demanding unreasonable sacrifices? How about that DMV license examiner who thinks his uniform authorizes him to be rude and to make you feel like a criminal just because you're there to comply with the law? Ever met a minister who thinks God has appointed him to cuttingly critique the lifestyles of the members of the congregation, right down to the choice of socks, slacks, shirt, or tie someone wears? Do you derive a certain wicked pleasure from humiliating your spouse by telling your friends, in your spouse's presence, about the embarrassing mistakes he or she has made?

This list could be endless. It would have been nice if we'd all learned at an early age that there are better ways to resolve our inner problems and that there is a better path for human beings to follow. Well, it's never too late to start doing what is right.

It's never too late to change things.

A Fresh Start

Chapter Ten

It's been quite a journey, a stretch of fifty years, from helping Mom raise up the car on that deadly winter night, all the way to the writing of this chapter. Now that I can look back from this vantage point, the hard knocks of my childhood are starting to fit into a much broader context. They haven't shrunk in significance, but they have found their place as one of many seasons in my life. The bad things really happened, but they aren't the *only* things that happened. They aren't even the *main* things that happened. God's plan for each of our lives covers a lot more ground, a lot more time than just that one, difficult season. The journey continues. His grace and mercies are new every morning and sufficient for each day.

But we have to wonder, Just what was that "one, difficult season" all about? What was the point? Well, speaking as a typical, nearsighted mortal, I can offer a few guesses.

Because I went through it, I can encourage and minister to others who have been there or who are there right now; and, as I've discovered, there are plenty of people who have abusive experiences that continue to dog them. God will use what you and I have gone through to help others find healing and deliverance from the wounds that still bring pain to their souls. Indeed, it may well be our wounds that provide the common ground on which other people can relate to us and we to them. As Brennan Manning writes in *Abba's Child*, "Grace and healing are communicated through the vulnerability of men and women who have been fractured and heartbroken by life."[1] Quoting Thornton Wilder's one-act play *The Angel That Troubled the Water*, based on John 5:1–4, Manning reminds us that in a strange sense, our woundedness qualifies us to point others to the Healer. "In Love's service, only wounded soldiers can serve."[2]

Since first giving my talk on the subject of wounded spirits, and as I've worked on this book, I've found it comforting to think that after thirty or forty years, the Lord and I can finally make some good use of all that trouble I went through. God does not waste an ounce of our pain or a drop of our tears; suffering doesn't come our way for no reason, and He seems especially efficient at using what we endure to mold our character. If we are malleable, He takes our bumps and bruises and shapes them into something beautiful. Maybe, because of what you and I have experienced, we can inspire a few changes in the way people think about and treat each other in this world.

I can see how God has worked through my wounds. Being a man of flesh, I could have turned out more careless and cruel in my conversation if I hadn't suffered some pain myself. Having been hurt by words, I have a better appreciation for what words can do. Wanting to be like Jesus, I try to watch my mouth; rather than lacing my conversation with sarcasm—an arrow with the tip only slightly dulled—I attempt to speak words of encouragement, and I try to uplift people I meet.

Similarly, having suffered at the hands of bullies, I've wanted very much not to be one. It's important to remember that many bullies who abuse others have been abused themselves. As Suellen and Paula Fried point out in *Bullies and Victims*, "They were not born bullies; they became bullies through their life experience."[3] Some were physically or verbally abused as children; many witnessed violence in the lives of their parents or other family members; most bullies have parents who have been or are too busy to give them the attention they need. Or perhaps they have been ignored by parents who are unaware of what is really going on in their children's lives. Sometimes even well-meaning parents are hard-pressed to spend the needed amount of quality time with their child, leaving the child with a sense of being unloved.

Often bullies have received inconsistent messages regarding discipline and boundaries. Bullies see threats where none exist; they see their anger as justified.[4] Because of these and other serious problems, bullies often end up as losers in life.

We don't rejoice in their hardship, nor do we condone their response to it, but if we develop an awareness that most bullies themselves are suffering wounded spirits, we will understand more about their inner pain, and we will have more compassion for the abusive person. We will recognize that often, just below the harsh exterior, there is a wounded child crying out to be noticed, and yes, to be loved.

So, I can see a lesson in the unhappy life of a bully: There is definitely a better life to be had by living life correctly, God's way, and there is a certain enabling grace God provides to help us do so. Consequently, I've sought God's wisdom and tried not to let this lesson pass me by.

On a practical level, having experienced how sour this world can be, I've tried to spread around as much sugar as I can. If I encounter a waitress having a bad day, I try to be as nice to her as I can be, and I usually leave a generous tip. It's a tangible way of saying, "You're doing a good job, and I appreciate you." Have you ever worked at a fast-food restaurant? If so, you probably have a greater appreciation for that young man or woman behind the counter who is trying to juggle several orders while customers wait impatiently. No doubt some irate customer has already yelled at my waitress for spilling something or counting the change wrong. I'd like to be the *nice* customer she has that day, the customer who gives *her* a break.

I try to use humor and display goodwill toward everyone with whom I do business, from bank clerks to telephone operators to FedEx delivery truck drivers. People appreciate kindness, and although virtue is its own reward, the Bible does promise that I will reap what I sow. Pass some sugar around, and Jesus will throw some sugar back to you, even more than you gave in the first place. It is, after all, the Lord Jesus whom we represent. As Saint Francis of Assisi put it, "Preach Christ . . . and if you must, use words."

Comforting others puts our pain into perspective. Having encountered others who have suffered multiple rapes, domestic violence, permanent disfigurement from disease or birth defect, molestation, and violent crime, I can tell myself, "Okay. You had some tough times, but be thankful. Compared to many people in this world, you had it easy."

I'm convinced that cruelty in and of itself is not fruitful, and to the fullest extent of my power, I won't allow it. Yes, God can make it all work together for good, but that's His miraculous way of redeeming a rotten situation, not His will for our behavior. I'm not impressed by the old argument that cruelty toughens us up for life. That's tantamount to saying it's right. Life is cruel enough by itself, thank you, with endless opportunities to suffer. Given that, one kind word or one encouraging touch teaches more lessons than one hundred cruelties.

We all have our "difficult seasons." Some of us are in the middle of one right now. We don't like them, of course, but they do have a way of finding their place in the overall scheme of our lives, welcome or not. There will be pain, and years afterward, there will still be questions. The sweet part of this is, as long as the Lord God is guiding your life, more years and more wisdom will bring a better perspective of what those tough times were all about. So trust God. He'll make things clear eventually.

I do see better days ahead. I intended this book to be a wake-up call, the cry of a lonely prophet, so to speak, but happily, I'm not the first one to raise this issue. As you'll see from the reading list in the back of this book, there are folks out there concerned with the problem of bullying and abuse, who want to advise and assist us in doing something about it. Check it out if you want to examine things further, and don't forget the Internet: Search the word *bully*, *bullies*, or *bullying*, and you'll be surprised how much material is available. You'll also be pleased, as I was, to find that much of the material is by or for those in education, meaning that our teachers and school administrators have plenty of practical resources from which to draw and no excuses for ignoring this matter ever again.

Maybe we're entering a new era in which bullying and the intimidation of other people are at last consigned to their rightful place alongside racism, hatemongering, drunk driving, littering, spitting in public, and passing gas at parties.

People are slowly waking up to the prolonged impact of the problem—that bullies in school often grow up to be bullies in the home, abusing their spouses and children and perpetuating the downward spiral. Bullies in the home leave the house and go to work, where they continue to abuse employees and coworkers. The cycle can only be stopped by a change of the heart, and that is precisely the place where God's power is more than sufficient to give people a fresh start. With other options exhausted, many people are finally beginning to give the spiritual solution some serious thought. Let's encourage more of that, and while we're at it, let's search our own hearts and instruct our children regarding what it means to be noble, to protect and help the weak, to love our neighbors—even the smaller, clumsy ones—as ourselves.

Most of all, we are called to be Jesus to the world around us, to demonstrate in word and deed, not simply in slogan, "What would Jesus do?" As we follow Christ and strive to be more like Him, may we also encourage people and share His love with each person we meet along the way. He is our Savior and Lord; He is the Answer for every broken heart, the one Answer we cannot live without—He is the Healer of the wounded spirit.

Endnotes

Chapter 4: Monsters on the Loose

1. Gavin DeBecker, "What the Columbine Report Didn't Tell You," APBnews.com, 19 May, 2000.

2. From Alan Prendergast, "The Missing Motive," from westword.com, originally published by *Westword*, 13 July 2000, copyright 2000 New Times, Inc. All rights reserved.

3. Gavin DeBecker, "What the Columbine Report Didn't Tell You."

4. Susan Greene, "Teen describes school life filled with taunts, abuse," DenverPost.com, 24 April 1999.

5. Ibid.

6. Suellen Fried and Paula Fried, *Bullies and Victims* (New York: M. Evans and Company, 1996), 87.

Chapter 5: Finding a Voice

1. Brent Curtis and John Eldredge, *The Sacred Romance* (Nashville: Thomas Nelson, 1997), 49.

2. Ibid.

Chapter 6: The Playground Parable

1. Gavin DeBecker, "What the Columbine Report Didn't Tell You," APBnews.com, 19 May, 2000.

2. From the tape series One Week in October, copyright 1999 by Ravi Zacharias, Ravi Zacharias International Ministries, 4725 Peachtree Corners Circle, Suite 250, Norcross, Georgia 30092.

3. John H. Hoover and Ronald Oliver, *The Bullying Prevention Handbook: A Guide for Principals, Teachers, and Counselors* (Bloomington, Ind.: National Educational Service, 1996), 96–97.

Chapter 7: Help for the Wounded

1. For more detailed reading on the subject of Christian morals and world-view, I heartily recommend the works of Ravi Zacharias, Francis Schaeffer, Josh McDowell, and C. S. Lewis.

Chapter 10: A Fresh Start

1. Brennan Manning, *Abba's Child* (Colorado Springs: NavPress, 1994), 26.

2. Ibid.

3. Suellen and Paula Fried, *Bullies and Victims*, 89.

4. Adapted from *Bullies and Victims*, 89–90.

Resources

Where You Can Find Help

The following list of resources is not exhaustive, nor is it necessarily a personal endorsement of the organizations listed, but it is a good place to start when you need help in dealing with bullying, abuse, intimidation, or the effects of other compulsive or addictive behaviors. It's normal to be nervous when reaching out for help, but don't let that hold you back. Be bold and courageous; contact someone on this list to help you. Begin today to do something that will bring about positive, Christ-centered change in your life, and in the lives of the people you love.

AMERICAN ASSOCIATION OF PASTORAL COUNSELORS
9504 A Lee Highway
Fairfax, VA 22031
phone: 703-385-6967

CANAAN LAND CHRISTIAN CENTER FOR WOMEN
2377 County Road 65
Marburg, AL 36051
phone: 334-365-9086
www.wrldnet.net

CANAAN LAND MINISTRIES
P.O. Box 310
Autaugaville, AL 36003-0310
phone: 334-365-2200
canaanland@bellsouth.net
Ministry to men.

CELEBRATION MINISTRIES
Al Denson
222 West Las Colinas Boulevard
Suite 1750
Irving, TX 75034
phone: 972-501-1456
aldenson.com
Christian musician, author, and minister offers Bible studies, public
school programs, and an on-line prayer request ministry.

CENTER FOR THE PREVENTION
OF SEXUAL AND DOMESTIC VIOLENCE
1914 N. 34th Street
Seattle, WA 98103
phone: 206-634-1903
Emergency: 800-562-6025

CHRISTIAN GROWTH CENTERS
P.O. Box 40
Hillsboro, NH 03244
phone: 603-464-5555
Specializes in helping young people who have been battered and
fragmented through broken homes, drugs, alcohol, etc.

DORCAS HOUSE
phone: 501-274-4022
Specializes in helping women and children who are victims of
domestic violence.

EXODUS INTERNATIONAL
P.O. Box 77652
Seattle, WA 98177
phone: 206-784-7799
fax: 206-784-7872
www.exodusintl.com

Equipping and uniting organizations to communicate freedom from homosexuality.

FAMILIES IN CRISIS, INC.
7320 Ohms Lane
Edina, MN 55435
phone: 612-893-1883

HOLY HIGHWAY
phone: 903-866-3300

Recommended for families with rebellious teenage girls.

LORD'S RANCH
Box 700
Warm Springs, AR 72478
phone: 870-647-2541
fax: 870-647-2337

LOST AND FOUND
phone: 303-697-5049

Help for those involved in drugs, alcohol, and sexual abuse.

MERCY MINISTRIES OF AMERICA
P.O. Box 111060
Nashville, TN 37222-1060
phone: 615-831-6987
fax: 615-315-9749
mercyministries.org

Mercy Ministries of America is a residential facility, provided free of charge, for troubled young women and unwed mothers between the ages of thirteen and twenty-eight, who are willing to commit six months to deal with life-controlling issues such as: pregnancy, drug and alcohol abuse, eating disorders, etc.

NATIONAL SCHOOL SAFETY CENTER
Pepperdine University
Malibu, CA 90263
phone: 805-373-9977

NEW CREATIONS
phone: 765-965-0099

Help for families with rebellious youth.

NEW HORIZONS MINISTRIES
1002 South 350 East
Marion, IN 46953-9502

Family and Christian character training.

NEW LIFE
phone: 800-NEW-LIFE

Counseling center and telephone crisis lines.

PARENTS ANONYMOUS

Contact:
Child Help USA
P.O. Box 630
Hollywood, CA 90028

A program for parents who already have or are afraid they might abuse their children.

RAPHA

4351 Shackleford Road
Norcross, GA 30093
phone: 800-383-HOPE
fax: 770-806-7641
www.raphacare.com

Rapha features Christ-centered, professional counseling for emotional and substance abuse, anxiety attacks, stress, unhealthy relationships, eating disorders, depression, drugs, alcohol, suicidal tendencies, etc.

REMUDA RANCH CENTER

One East Apache Street
Wickenburg, AZ 85390
phone: 800-445-1900

SHELTERWOOD

12550 Zuni Street
Westminster, CO 80234
phone: 800-584-5005
shelterwood.org

"Restoring families through Christian relationships."

TEEN CHALLENGE INTERNATIONAL
P.O. Box 1015
Springfield, MO 65801
phone: 800-814-5728
http://www.teenchallenge.com

Specializes in seeking spiritual solutions to addictive behavior patterns.

WALTER HOVING HOME
P.O. Box 194
Garrison, NY 10525
phone: 914-424-3674

"Rebuilding lives shattered by drugs and alcohol, and other life-controlling problems."

Web Sites

(Please note: This is not necessarily an endorsement of these sites, or the information included on them; however, this brief list will give you a place to start in searching for other resources.)

http://www.successunlimited.co.uk
  (Dealing primarily with bullying in the United Kingdom, this site also includes a section on bullying in the United States.)

http://www.mobbing-usa.com
  (The terms "mobbing" and "bullying" are often used interchangeably in the U. S.)

http://www.bullybusters.org
  (This site charges for their services. The other listings provide free information.)

http:// stopbullying.com
  (A one-stop resource on dealing with childhood bullying and teasing.)

Recommended Reading List

1. Bernall, Misty. *She Said Yes: The Unlikely Martydom of Cassie Bernall.* Farmington, N.Y.; Nashville: Copublishers, Plough and Word, 1999.

2. Curtis, Brent, and John Eldredge. *The Sacred Romance.* Nashville: Thomas Nelson, 1997.

3. Fried, Suellen, and Paula Fried. *Bullies and Victims.* New York: M. Evans and Company, 1996.

4. Gaddis, Patricia Riddle. *Battered But Not Broken.* Valley Forge, Pa.: Judson Press, 1996.

5. Kroeger, Catherine Clark, and James R. Beck. *Women, Abuse, and the Bible.* Grand Rapids: Baker, 1996.

6. Manning, Brennan. *Abba's Child.* Colorado Springs: NavPress, 1994.

7. McDowell, Josh, and Bob Hostetler. *Right From Wrong.* Dallas: Word, 1994.

8. Zacharias, Ravi. *A Shattered Visage: The Real Face of Atheism.* Grand Rapids: Baker, 1993.

9. Zacharias, Ravi. *Can Man Live Without God.* Dallas: Word, 1994.

10. Zacharias, Ravi. *Deliver Us from Evil.* Nashville: Word, 1996.

The Oath

Master of supernatural thrillers Frank Peretti brings us *The Oath*, a chilling novel of murder and mystery. A 110-year-old town has fallen prey to an unexplainable predator and no one wants to talk about it. Layer upon layer, this serpentine plot peels away at the ramifications of an ancient oath.

The Visitation

Sightings of angels, messianic images, a weeping crucifix with the power to heal, and a self-proclaimed prophet bring the national media and droves of curious people to this small Northwestern town. The startling secret behind this visitation pushes one man into a supernatural confrontation that will forever change the lives of everyone involved.

Also in *The Wounded Spirit* Product Line Available February 2001

- The *Wounded Spirit* Workbook
- The *Wounded Spirit* Leader's Guide
- The *Wounded Spirit* Curriculum (includes one workbook, one leader's guide, and one 45-minute video)

WORD PUBLISHING
www.wordpublishing.com